Keep Going

Aging Gratefully and Surviving Heartbreak
and Challenges with Resilience,
Appreciation, Humour and Faith.

Diane M. Waterman

*All great spirituality is about what we do with our pain.
If we do not transform our pain, we will
transmit it to those around us.*

Richard Rohr

Other books by Diane:

When Lilacs Bloom (2013)
You Have to Go Now (2017)
The Married Man (2020)

Keep Going
Copyright © 2025 Diane M. Waterman
dianemwaterman@hotmail.com

All rights reserved. No part of this book may be used or reproduced by any means, graphic, electronic, or mechanical, including photocopying, recording, taping or by any information storage retrieval system without the written permission of the author except in the case of brief quotations embodied in critical articles and reviews.

Cover Design: Agata Broncel, bukovero.com
Typesetting: Edge of Water Designs

ISBN:
978-1-0694062-0-0

For MacKenzie xo
And for all those who fight hard to stay.

TABLE OF CONTENTS

Chapter 1	Revelation	1
Chapter 2	Therapy is Healing	9
Chapter 3	Loving You	18
Chapter 4	A Blessing at Sixty-Five	23
Chapter 5	Precious Surprise	25
Chapter 6	Aging and Humour	28
Chapter 7	Lessons of Humility	40
Chapter 8	God Works in Mysterious Ways	52
Chapter 9	Near Bottom	64
Chapter 10	Time for Change	71
Chapter 11	Free As a Bird	85
Chapter 12	The Married Man	91
Chapter 13	The Shoe Drops	99
Chapter 14	Physical Touch	119
Chapter 15	The Blue Orb	136
Chapter 16	The Bridge	144
Chapter 17	More Humility	152
Chapter 18	Despair, Repair and the Universe	163
Chapter 19	The Read	167
Chapter 20	Forgiveness is Freedom	172
Chapter 21	Thankful for my Worse Days	184

Chapter 22	We Love You MacKenzie	194
Chapter 23	Mental Health Awareness	208
About Diane		225

THE COVER PHOTO

The cover photo is of me and my 3 sisters taken in 1964. This photo is significant in my story and is why I chose it as my cover. This book being sort of a sequel to my book *You Have to Go Now* is why I wanted to use another photo of me with my sisters that connects both books as well. My sisters were so important in my life and are forever a big part of my history that is now missing for me. I still feel their loss every day. With two of them passing away in their fifties and my youngest sister Faye being lost to the drug world for much of her life, my life suddenly became very lonely without them. The cover photo has been my screen saver on my laptop for many years now. My younger brother, by ten years, was not yet born in the time of this story line. I love him dearly. From left to right in the photo is me, Mona, Donna and baby sister Faye. I changed Faye's name in my last memoir to Maye to protect her. I feel she is okay now with me using her real name. She deserves to be acknowledged properly. I miss my siblings every day. xoxoxoxo

The back cover photo is my granddaughter MacKenzie's hand holding a butterfly and a dragon fly. All creatures big and small were drawn to her beautiful spirit here as I know they still are in the spirit world. RIP, sweetheart. xo

THE TITLE

I had the urge to write another book three years ago but didn't have any idea what to write about or if I should do another fiction or true story? I did know I was going through a lot in recent years and thought writing about my struggles might not only help me to heal but others as well who may connect to them. I finally decided to do another true story and I wanted it to be a sequel of sorts to *You Have to Go Now*. I feel each book can stand on its own. You don't have to read the first one to read the second. They each have their own stories.

I was talking to my son Jeffrey around this time and I told him a little bit about my idea for a new book and that I couldn't come up with the title. The title has always been the inspiration for me behind the books I write. I can't start to write a book without having the title first. Jeffrey suggested to try asking my higher self during mediation and see what happens. It sounded like a good idea to me.

During my meditation the next day I asked my higher self to please help me come up with a title for my new book. I didn't go to sleep during the meditation but I was in that place of total peace. As I was about to open my eyes I was suddenly hearing a soft feminine voice gently and clearly say, "Keep going, keep going, keep going." My first thought was 'Is that my voice?' It didn't sound like me. I realized it was my higher-self speaking to me. What we sometimes call our intuition.

I had heard it at other times in my past.

A smile came across my face as I realized how many times during my hard days did I say those two little powerful words to help me Keep Going! I am certain I am not the only person who has uttered those two words as a mantra in times of pain and struggle. Those two little words have literally kept me alive. This was the perfect title! I thanked the Universe and my higher self for the title and later thanked my son for the suggestion. I knew from that moment it had to be the title of my new book and I was suddenly inspired to start writing again.

I chose to use the word gratefully instead of gracefully in the subtitle. It is not a typo. I used gracefully at first but then changed it because life is not always graceful. Staying grateful is more important to me.

THINGS I AM IN LOVE WITH AND LIVE FOR...

I love God. I love my children and grandchildren more than life itself. I love my friends. I love belly laughs. I love good hugs and kisses. I love kindness. I love service for others. I love loyalty. I love surviving challenges. I love learning. I love having faith.

I love the warmth of the sun on my face. I love sunrises and sunsets. I love the sound of a loved one's voice over the phone. I love sitting on a park bench, closing my eyes and listening to the rustling of the trees. I love the sound of the birds singing their unique melodies. I love people watching. I love eating a home-cooked meal and watching The Voice and American Idol, anything musical. I love old movies.

I love walking every day. I love nature. I love the ocean. I love star gazing. I love the moon. I love the rain. I love the smell of a baby. I love the smell of baking, especially at Christmas time. I love feeling my best physically and mentally and getting dolled up to go out dancing on a Saturday night. I love playing my guitar and singing.

I love co-creating with God. I love art, writing, reading, movies, music and dance. I love that I have learned spiritual energy healing. I love meditation and yoga. I love affection. I love making love, with someone I love. I love a nice glass of Chardonnay. I love chocolate cake. I love me and I love you.

Chapter 1

REVELATION

In July of 1964, four little girls ages 4, 6, 7 and 8 and their parents were travelling from Goose Bay, Labrador to the island of Newfoundland to visit their extended family for the summer holidays. The four little girls were all close in age and were dressed the same in their matching summer dresses, coats and little white purses. Their ash blond hair was all cut the same bob style by their mother. They were far from rich but these little girls were well dressed, clean and clearly taken care of and loved.

As they entered their grandparent's home in Clarke's Head, Gander Bay, Newfoundland they were surrounded by their loving extended family. There was so much excitement in the air! All four girls were standing in the center of that love filled kitchen while being swooned over by their aunts, uncles and grandparents. Quickly one aunt stood up and swooped up one little girl into her arms saying "This is my girl." Then another aunt within seconds swept up the second and then the third aunt did the same with the third sister. Within a matter of seconds three sisters disappeared from the center of the kitchen. The forth was left standing there for what seemed like forever but in reality was only about ten seconds. Each second that ticked by felt like an eternity to this child. It wasn't because she was last that changed that little girl but because it took what felt like forever for anyone to choose her that had changed her perception of herself that day. Without even knowing she buried that uncomfortable feeling deep in her heart right away. Finally with great relief, a special aunt stood up and took her hand to come join her and sit on her knee.

That little seven year old girl was me. Without being aware I buried what I felt in that moment for the next thirty years. I did feel suddenly that there was something about me that my family, that I loved dearly, didn't like about me. Let me make it clear, that was my perception as a child, not theirs.

There would have been no words for me to describe how I felt as a child and I had no way to express it. I just knew I suddenly felt uncomfortable. It was no fault whatsoever of my families. I was learning a life lesson at a very young age. I know no one would purposely hurt me and I feel beyond loved today and always have felt loved by my extended family, just not in that moment. I love them beyond measure and they have been a constant support system for me in my life. It was simply a moment in time when I perceived something as any sensitive, seven year old would have. It stuck with me more than I ever knew probably because I am an empath.

Many years later my sisters and I were living in Fort McMurray, married and raising our own families. I was turning thirty-six. My sister Donna had come to visit me and gave me a photo of the four of us sisters taken on that same day that we had arrived at our grandparent's home when we were children. It was a gift of love that was surrounded by a small gold frame. I was ecstatic to have it! I had no prior memory of seeing the photo before then.

After my sister left I started remembering clearly that moment in time. The memories suddenly began flooding back of me and my siblings standing in the center of my grandmother's kitchen. The feeling of being very alone suddenly stood out. I felt something that made me instantly sad. I swallowed it and shrugged it off.

That same night my sisters and a few of our close friends were gathering at my aunt and uncles for coffee. When I showed up everyone was already sitting around the table. The usual chatter was going on between the women with lots of laughter. That was how it was whenever we gathered. There was never any shortage of fun and catching up. As I sat there taking it all in, I felt something was building up in my chest. It suddenly felt like my heart was swelling and hurting. It felt very uncomfortable.

When someone asked how I was doing I started to share with them the little story about my gift from Donna that day and how much I had loved it. Except the moment I tried to talk about it I broke down. I was completely startled and shocked at how I suddenly fell apart! Every time I tried to speak I sobbed more and more deeply. They were all asking me what was wrong but I couldn't blubber more than a word or two out at a time. The pain in my heart was overwhelming! It was a wound so deep I felt like my chest was cracking open. I made a gesture with my hand to let them know, just give me a minute. I had to just lay my arms on the table, lay my head down and let myself cry it out. I couldn't believe that something so minor in all reality had hurt my heart so much.

Now in my sixties I understand more clearly the effect of that moment in time and how it has moulded me over the years. The beauty and privilege of aging for sure is growth and wisdom.

That need I have to be independent, the pride that I have in all that I do and the fight and will that I have had over the years, I know now some of it stems from that one moment in time almost sixty years ago. Even when failing, which are necessary lessons to make us stronger and wiser, I value myself. I have for a long time now. That's why I won't settle for less than I deserve in life. Sometimes it took a lot of work and there have been many battles and steps in growth when I've been side tracked and lost, but I am still here stronger than ever because of that little girl that just won't quit.

This fight I felt all throughout my life to feel worthy and survive anything all came from those ten seconds of standing alone in that wonderful, love filled kitchen. Most children would not even notice or be affected by such a minor thing but I was for a reason. It has kept me alive.

I just also realized in this very moment while I am writing, that I wasn't standing alone at all. I just had a huge AHA moment and I'm now going to share it. This happens to me often when I write. Wow!

Life really is about our perception of just about any situation. We can change a negative feeling to a positive one if we simply change how we look at it. I do this often in life in general but had not turned this memory around until this very moment. What an important lesson I am sharing now for all of us.

I actually see myself now as standing OUT in that moment in the center of my grandmother's kitchen and not standing alone at all. God wanted me to stand out and to shine in the spotlight for a moment longer because He saw something in me that I wouldn't see for decades to come. He saw a survivor! What a revelation this is for me!

My heart clearly needed this lesson when I was seven to survive all that was ahead of me in my life and to make me stronger. It made that little girl a fighter that wanted to prove herself time and time again. You really can't be a survivor if you give up easily. Herein lies my strength and the tears are now pouring…

One thing I've become pretty good at in past years is turning a negative into a positive and writing often makes me see things more clearly to see the positive. It is truly all about perception. Clarity often happens in the moment as I write. It can take a day or years sometimes before we can see light in the darkness. And what I had perceived as a seven year old wasn't reality but my truth at the time through a child's eyes that in the end would only make me stronger. God knew I would need it. What a beautiful moment this is for me and I am grateful for my aunties that did that for me without even knowing. My heart is overwhelmed with love for each of them! If that one little moment had not happened I don't know if I would have grown up to have such a will to fight and Keep Going. My heart is grateful!

I know in this moment I am co-creating to come to these clarities. It comes from God, the Universe, Source, whatever you choose to call it that helps us learn, grow and heal. That's what inspirational writing is. I truly believe that my writing without the inspiration and creativity I receive from beyond the veil would never happen. I am grateful for the clarity it gives me to now share with you. It is truly a gift for us all.

I was worthy the day I was born and will always be worthy. We all are! That moment in my grandmother's kitchen was meant to make me toughen up. It would take pure strength from my own will to get through all that was before my little seven year old self in the coming years. I had to toughen up or I would not survive what my future held. And I would have to do it many times, with God's help.

As we all know growth and learning never ends no matter how old we become. For many years growing up I called myself the ugly duckling in the family. It made sense to me now why I felt that way for so long. It is no longer my perception as the woman I am today and hasn't been for many years now, even with my aging body. Someone had to be last and what a blessing it was to be me.

That little 4 x 4 photo given to me by my sis and the memories it evoked were meant to happen. Everything has a purpose or reason in our journey. That strong will to prove myself has always made me want to do better and to be better in my choices in life. I've had many struggles to learn from which made me both compassionate and sensitive to others that suffer. I was born an empath and that is my strength and often my weakness. It is truly the heart of an empath who loves the most and suffers the most.

As a senior now I have learned one of the most important lessons in life is that it doesn't matter if anyone else chooses me first along this journey as long as I choose me first to take care of and to love. This is not meant in an egotistical way at all, it is meant to mean that I take care of my own well-being first in order to then take care of others. I couldn't teach anything of any value without doing life that way. Not only was this still hard to do sometimes, because life throws us new lessons to learn all the time, but that I have had to learn to do it again and again to get to where I am now and to truly love who I am as a human being.

Little did that seven year old girl know that her future challenges would not only empower her but from what I've been told, others as well?

Chapter 2

THERAPY IS HEALING

I came to realize in my mid-thirties that I needed emotional help. I had a lot of work to do on me. It would take a lot more courage than I knew I had at the time. I needed to find and take back that free spirited young girl that I once was. Even without knowing that I had placed a negative outlook on how I perceived myself and how others saw me back then, I still loved life in general. It wasn't until I was thirty nine that I finally took the steps that would start my journey towards really healing and loving me. I had very little self-love, if any before then. Not because of that moment in my grandmother's kitchen, although my perception of it still dwelled somewhere inside me at the time, but because of some of the bad choices I had made over the years that had damaged my spirit. I had lived through some very hard struggles up to then and still had a lot to learn before I could get to a point of healing old hurts from my past.

I would start my journey of healing by entering therapy at thirty nine years old. It was at that age that I started feeling

Diane M. Waterman

I was meant to do something meaningful with my life. I just couldn't figure out what it was. I had a lot of work to do to heal me from multiple hurts before I could begin to really understand who I was. I felt being a mom was amazing and what I was made for but yet there was a yearning for more. I had not been taking care of number one for many years.

After going for ten months of excellent counselling I suddenly no longer saw myself as that ugly duckling. There were a series of things that I did at that time that was life changing for me and helped me in my journey of taking care of and loving me. I received more knowledge and growth in my late thirties and early forties than in all the years before. I couldn't read enough books on subjects of healing and growth.

When I talk about loving me I am referring to the inside. In my opinion the outside will always reflect the inside no matter how we look physically. After a lot of determination and work I was suddenly feeling that bliss. I took more risks those years than I ever did in my entire life and the growth would only continue from there. That little girl was suddenly blossoming into a confidant woman!

I woke up every morning for months and the first thing I would do when I looked in a mirror was to say 'I love you.' It took a few months of repeating it daily and before long I actually started to believe it and feel it. Something deep inside me was changing. That one daily practice alone changed so much for me and my confidence back then. Forgiving me for my bad choices took a lot of work as well. Only I could turn around all those negative beliefs I had about myself for so many years. This was great homework and practices for me taught to me by my wonderful counsellor. I learned so much from the books I chose to read as well. Practicing positive thoughts every day was the key to any future success I may have in loving my life. There are so many self-help books out there now you can go online and choose any and not go wrong. We all start somewhere. Choose what you feel most connected to.

Having a mother who I adored but couldn't show me any affection also made me feel unlovable as a child. I was and still am an affectionate person. That need has always been there for me. It took me years to realize that was just the way my mom was. It wasn't anything against me. We were just different that way. Mom also grew up in a different time when there wasn't a lot of affection shown. She took good care of us and showed us love in other ways. I feel I did inherit her strength and hard work ethics. I am so grateful for that.

I went on to marry a man who beat it in my head constantly that I was worthless. This only confirmed what I already had perceived for so many years that I wasn't lovable or worthy of love. I was more drawn to men who didn't know how to love and my choices only confirmed for me what I already felt deep down. I didn't realize this about me of course because I was too young and didn't learn enough yet. I buried a lot.

Truthfully looking back, if I had any confidence at all I wouldn't have allowed this daily emotional abuse to go on for nearly twenty years.

All of this along with my seven year old self unconsciously believing I wasn't lovable made it inconceivable to me that I may be intelligent or attractive in any way. BUT, there was always a knowing and awareness somewhere deep down that I was smarter than I was made to believe I was. My spirit knew. I just needed to heal and reveal my true self. I was told daily how dumb and ugly I was in some way by my ex. My esteem was beat down more and more over those years. What I found out through therapy was I hated me more than him because I allowed it to go on for so long out of so many fears instilled in me by a bully and there was deep shame I carried for my lack of courage to leave.

By then there were decades of negative self-talk that I had to work hard at to turn around in my brain. It doesn't happen overnight and even when you feel you are close, the future will throw you more negativity that can trigger you and set you back. It's a work in progress for life to stay aware and hold onto that love for you because life's circumstances and others will try and take it away. Life can bring you down again and again and make you fight even harder to hang onto that wisdom you've now learned. You have to keep remembering your value no matter what the situation. The key to wellness is to stay aware of how we feel inside. It is our compass to how we are doing.

Keep Going

I had a ton of work to do. The majority of damage was done to my heart, body and soul in that one choice at the age of nineteen of choosing someone abusive to date and then marry at twenty one. I take full responsibility for that choice. The damage it did to me and my children would take a lot of deep reflection, understanding, compassion and forgiveness for me and somehow for him as well. It would take many years of work. I had to try and see my ex in a different light as well and feel for him and his journey. I had to dig real deep for that.

I was very spirited and seemed to be happy for most of my teenage years, despite the deeper feelings I wasn't yet aware from going through other traumas. Marrying who I married completely broke my happy spirit. The work I had to do at that time was ongoing to change my outlook of me and to heal from so much abuse. My ex wasn't willing to put in the work which along with everything else led to the inevitable divorce almost twenty years later.

Telling my kids positive things I saw in them to constantly build up their esteem against the negative energy in our home was a full time job. Among so much darkness I tried to be the light of hope for them to be happy and kind hearted human beings. With therapy I found a flicker of hope that with hard work we would all survive the damage that had been inflicted over such a long period of time.

Leaving an abusive man of almost twenty years back in 1996

was just the beginning of what I could do to improve my life and my children's lives in the long run. We have all learned that abuse of any kind is not okay. I still had so much to learn and do in those years. With a lot of work and determination I was suddenly getting stronger and happier than I had been in the twenty years prior. I had finally found the courage to leave.

It was a very exciting and also a very scary time for me to be free of so much negativity. There was pure relief from what had been a huge build-up of not only hate and anger towards him but for me as well. Forgiving me for being weak and allowing it to harm me and my family was the most important thing I had to work on. The physical abuse towards me was absorbed weekly in the first seven years until I learned when to shut up and not talk back, but the constant insults and emotional abuse over the years ran even deeper. Healing twenty years of this would be ongoing and I was more than ready to move forward into the unknown.

Divorcing my ex in 1997 was a very positive time of growth in my life. I suddenly felt like a new woman. I finally broke free, almost! He was still lurking for years to come until I moved to Edmonton in 2004. Even then I had to be around him for the sake of my kids. I also had to get over feeling like a failure because I divorced. In the end I felt it was a positive for me and my family. I stepped out of so many fears at that time. Being told all the time when I threatened to leave him, "Look at you, who would hire you? Look at you, who would want you?" had kept me under his thumb for far too long by stripping away any sense of confidence that I might have had. And there were threats when I talked about leaving him like, "I must clean my gun." There was so much fear instilled in me over the years I felt it would take a miracle for me to get out. I had longed for so long for someone to help me. I came to realize through therapy that nobody was going to save me but me. I give my therapist all the credit for helping me believe in me.

I knew in my heart I had tried everything under the sun to make our marriage work but it takes two and he did not want to face anything that was hard to heal for him. That's his life's path. I have no ill feelings for him now. He was hurt too somewhere along the way.

Forgiving me was even harder because I knew my choices had hurt not only me but my children. Being a good mom was so important to me and I felt I was the worse mom keeping myself and my children in such a toxic environment for so many years out of fear.

Healing all of that 'stuff' for me at the age of thirty nine was the key to my self-love and saving me and my children the best way I knew how. Divorce is not always a bad thing. I was very happy to be free of the daily drama. All of my children have had therapy and I believe have led better lives because of that and that one big decision I made back then. I can't imagine our lives if I didn't make that choice. It doesn't mean any of our lives are perfect, far from it but I know none of us will allow abusive behaviour to stay in our lives for long. It takes time to know people.

My therapist said to me when I told him I was filing for a divorce, "Diane this is huge what you are doing. You are breaking the chain that has gone on for many generations." The more I learned about my own extended family the more I know this to be true. There was a history of abusive men in my family tree and I did break that chain at least for my family and hopefully future generations. I grew up with an angry yet loving and affectionate father. As much as I loved my father, the contrast was very confusing for me of what was accepting.

My therapist also told me to be careful when I told him I was leaving my husband. He knew it was a very dangerous time for me but I stepped through all my fears and did it anyway.

We were in the middle of yet another argument when I told my ex I was leaving just four months after my ten months of therapy had ended. I looked him straight in the eyes and said with all confidence and conviction, "You can go ahead and kill me if you want because I would rather be dead than to spend another day living with you!" For the first time in twenty years it was him that now showed fear because for the first time he knew it wasn't just a threat. He knew I meant it. After a lot of therapy and daily work I was ready and determined to

Keep Going

make a positive change for me and my three children before my fortieth birthday, and I did.

One thing I changed my outlook on that was very important at that time was, although I was victimized for many years I would never see myself as a victim ever again. No matter what other challenges I would have to grow from in the future there was a knowing deep down inside of me that I would always come out as a survivor.

Who was this woman I was just getting to know?!

Chapter 3

LOVING YOU

When we don't feel worthy as children we will certainly attract more negative in our lives without even knowing why. If we choose to learn and grow from our past instead of staying stuck in it that is positive and amazing growth!

I still make bad choices sometimes that teaches me something new about myself and that forces me to dig deep to find my courage. Not all days can be good but at this point in my life I can honestly say I've had way more good days than bad, and for that I am grateful. The contrast of bad times teaches us to really appreciate the good times. My life has not been boring, that's for sure. I have had plenty of ups and downs.

I did stuff my feelings with food for the years I was married. It was also used against me and added to my self-loathing. I had gained more weight after having the three children as well. I fought to lose it and yo-yo dieted for much of that time trying to get it off but it never lasted. Food was my comfort. I lost 100 pounds of what I had gained over the twenty years I was married during my therapy and have pretty much kept it under control for the past 28 years now. I do fluctuate a little between summer and winter when not being as active. Taking control of the bad eating habits showed how determined I was to heal and have a better life for me and my children. I always wanted to set a better example for them and I worked hard to do just that in finally taking care of number one. I started to learn who I really was. This is so important! I believe no matter what age our children are they absorb our actions, not our words. That old cliché is true. Turning all this around took more strength and courage than I ever imagined I had inside of me.

Many times when I was married I could have taken a way out in those very dark times and there have been times since but I just can't ever seem to give up. I thank God every day now for these lessons of compassion, stubbornness and discipline that have kept me alive today. I am stronger for it.

We all have a choice in what we accept for ourselves in life. Walking away from toxic people is the best thing we can do for our own sanity and well-being. That does not mean there is no love.

I have a wonderfully supportive and big extended family and like them I try my best to never hurt anyone intentionally. It is not possible to be aware all the time of every little action we do or everyone's life would be perfect all the time. That is not reality. I am sure I have hurt people many times too. God knows

I've ticked my kids off plenty of times. I work on letting them walk their own paths and to stop being the 'mother hen' as they became adults. Now that's a challenge. *chuckles* They are always our babies in a mom's mind no matter how old they are. I feel they have taught me a lot and I have certainly let go of worrying as much about them in letting them create their own paths and learn from it as I have. That has not been easy sometimes but I am much better at it. They are all intelligent and loving people that I am proud of and they all know I'm here when they need me.

My experience has been we will not draw the best of all of our deepest desires to us until we get in a good head space and heart space. The best way to live is to be in the moment as much as possible. Enjoy the good days and learn from the bad. Life is a constant flow of ups and downs and the sooner we let the bad flow through us and move on, the better.

To share my own experiences and words of self-awareness to help others has become my greatest purpose in life now. It always makes me happy to help people. If we choose to be miserable and complaining all the time we are attracting more things to complain about. The law of attraction proves this. Without a doubt what we believe is what we will manifest. Moving beyond my past, other than to heal and teach what I've learned, has been healthy for me. I still had plenty of hard struggles coming in my future. My experience and great will has no doubt helped me survive them. Many will not make it through struggles without self-destruction or death. I've worked hard to never go down that road.

Being an empath I feel I have to push myself and work even harder than many when there is heartbreak. When I get past the hard times and still have my head on straight is when I realize how strong I really am. We simply don't give ourselves enough credit sometimes.

After my divorce I went to work in the jewelry business and had many happy years still growing and learning. I loved my new life and loved my freedom. By the time I was 47 I had three beautiful grandchildren already. They brought so much joy and happiness in my life. I saw them often when I was living in Fort McMurray back then. When I moved away to St. Albert and then into Edmonton in 2004 I didn't see them as often but would see them more later on once my children followed me to Edmonton five years later. We spent a lot of family time together and I have some wonderful memories of those times I got to cook big dinners for my family again.

Over time as I aged I was having a harder time struggling with fibromyalgia. Eventually I had to quit my job I loved at 55 not being able to work on my feet nine hours a day anymore. Even part time was difficult. I tried hard to keep working but it was no longer my path.

Now at almost sixty-five I feel better than ever as I am

constantly learning to take better care of me physically and mentally. I grieved leaving my job in jewelry for some time, missing the social part the most. Everything happens for a reason and I would soon learn God had a more fulfilling path for me in the future of writing. The journey of life, love and lessons never ends. And what better extension of love is there than receiving yet another grandchild.

Chapter 4

A BLESSING AT SIXTY-FIVE

Today is September 25th 2021, my 65th birthday. How blessed I feel to have made it this far! My four children called me to wish me a happy birthday which always makes me happy! (I had a child before I was married that was adopted. The full story is in *You Have To Go Now*. We were blessed to meet when I was 44 and Jason was 25. It went well and we are still in contact today.)

I received a message from my friend Dinah saying she would come to see me on her days off. I received many birthday wishes and messages through social media from family and friends near and far and I got a call from my long-time friend Colette who moved away many years ago. I hadn't seen her for ten years but she did come to see me the following month and we got to have a fun filled 24 hours together celebrating both of our birthdays. I will always need and appreciate these special connections in my life.

My greatest and for sure the best birthday gift anyone could only dream of on their birthday is to receive a brand new baby granddaughter. My youngest daughter Hanna gave birth to her first baby at the age of thirty. My daughter is living four hours away. Because of covid I couldn't be there for the birth. That was heartbreaking for me but necessary at the time.

My granddaughter arrived five days early at 5:06 pm and she is a beauty! I am filled with so much emotion as I write this. I had no doubt in my mind that she would arrive on my birthday and she didn't let Nanny down. I prayed for it and even went as far as manifesting it. I couldn't imagine a better gift to receive as a grandmother. Long after I am gone she will hopefully always remember my love for her on her birthday.

I have been face timing with our new baby girl and her Mom every day until I get to hold her in my arms. We had to be extra cautious because of covid 19 of course but I couldn't wait. Turning sixty-five on the day she was born will always be a day of much joy for me to remember forever. It was an amazing birthday and a special gift for this now official senior.

Chapter 5

PRECIOUS SURPRISE.

On October 20th 2021 at 6:15 pm I was making supper in my kitchen when suddenly there was a loud knocking on my door. My front entrance is right next to my kitchen. I looked out my peephole but couldn't see anyone. I suddenly felt a little fearful. I couldn't think of anyone who would be at my door. I live in a secure building. No one can get in without a key. I knew it wasn't the caretakers knock.

My heart was racing a little as I called out "Who is it?" No answer, but I suddenly heard a dog whimpering. I thought 'OH MY GOD IT'S BALTO!!' He was my daughters little dog. I pulled the door open and Balto whipped past my legs running around in frenzy as he always did when he would visit me. (Balto has since passed. Rip little man.)

There was no one else in site until I looked down. There was a car seat sitting directly in front of my door with my brand new granddaughter sleeping in it. She was wrapped warmly and looked so cozy! I was sooooo excited!! I wasn't expecting to go see her for a few more weeks. It had been decided we would give it some time with all the restrictions in place then and for my daughter to have time to adjust and recuperate. Well, surprise, surprise!

My daughter stepped out from hiding outside of my door grinning from ear to ear and her fiancé stepped out from the other side grinning as well. I looked at Hanna and I swore half laughing and half crying. It wasn't nice dropping the F bomb but when in shock I am not responsible for what I say. We held onto each other tight and cried! Her fiancé grabbed the car seat and brought baby girl inside. I hugged him and just kept saying, "I can't believe it, I can't believe it!!" When I came to my senses I took my supper off the stove and proceeded to put on my mask and wash my hands to hold my brand new precious grandchild.

When Hanna placed her in my arms more tears fell. I was crying and Hanna was crying. It felt a little awkward to me at first because it had been ten years since I held a baby but how sweet it was as I soon positioned her in a comfortable place in my arms. Her eyes were looking straight into mine as we connected. She has golden blond hair and soft pink skin. Holding her took me back right away to holding her mom as a baby. There is no better blessing in life. I got to spend that evening and all of the next day with them before they left to go back to Edmonton. I know it was hard on my daughter to come on that trip with a small baby. Hanna was really tired.

Keep Going

I appreciated it more than she will ever know. It meant the world to me!

Chapter 6

AGING AND HUMOUR

One of the nice things I feel I have always had going for me is my sense of humour. My dad had a great sense of humour. Becoming a grandma again is definitely one of the sweetest and most beautiful benefits of aging but God only knows, everything about getting older is not fun. Quite frankly it can suck! Me being me, I have to try and see the positives of it and try and turn some of the negatives into humour.

Some things we just have to laugh at and laughter keeps us young. No matter how hard life becomes I will often use humour to help me through it. I have no problem laughing at myself and I have been told by others I am witty and funny. I love hearing that. It is also my favourite quality in anyone else.

My whole family had and has great humour but Donna and I could see humour in a rock. With all three of my sisters I can only imagine how our conversations would have been about growing old together and all the changes we would go through while aging. We would have supported and laughed our way through it all. I often have a chuckle with my brother about growing old. He does have the advantage of being ten years younger. Still, we both feel changes. I tell myself often that age is just a number to convince myself I can stay young forever, in my mind at least. *chuckles*

Losing Donna at the young age of 51, Mona at the age of 57, and my Mom at 56 were not only devastating but life changing. My youngest sister Faye (who is still alive) I lost to drug addiction. I still have some contact off and on with Faye but I haven't seen her in more than 27 years. Part of her story I told in my book, *You Have to Go Now*. In 2016 I lost my dad at the age of 80. My brother is thankfully still alive and living in Newfoundland. Our relationship has been strained at times over the years. He also struggled with drug addiction and sadly there were times I didn't hear from him for months at a time or even years. He is doing better now and we stay in touch and love each other. I am proud of his progress in living healthier.

The years when we were all together in happier times I loved to play practical jokes on my family and would be in tears of laughter just setting them up. It was never anything big or lavish, just fun. My oldest sister Mona, by ten and a half months, was more serious and I am sure embarrassed sometimes by us younger sisters in all of our silliness. Sometimes she would just look at us shaking her head but still with a grin on her face. We loved to laugh together. I miss that more than anything.

These fond memories have never left me. I never dreamed I would be growing old without my sisters.

Every day I still get to live and experience I feel is a blessing and I want to represent them well. My mother and two sisters never lived to see me publish a book but my baby sister Faye has read the last three and she told me that she is very proud of me. It meant so much to me to hear that from her. I'm proud of her too for trying to do better in her life. She has tried. That's all I can ask and I still pray for a miracle for her. I'm proud of her talents and honesty about herself.

Me and Faye have cried and laughed sharing memories of our childhood in more recent years. After reading *You Have to Go Now* she said, "There is a reason we are the last two sisters living. I was meant to heal through reading your book." I can't tell you how much that touched me. I cried like a baby. My purpose for writing it was fulfilled just by that statement alone. As time goes on I hear from her less and less again. I love her and keep her in my prayers.

As for the physical aging process, I see the wrinkles deepening on my face, my skin thinning and going softer day by day in these past few years. I have accepted the age spots making an appearance everywhere on my body and the veins showing more in my hands and feet as each year passes. I am embracing each one and counting my blessings that I am still here to witness the process.

I get dry eyes and dry mouth. I have a glass of water close by as I sleep every night, glasses close by because I wear progressive lenses. Everything is blurry without them.

My mind is still good, despite a little memory loss sometimes but things usually come back to me in a short time. I feel there will always be stresses popping up. Learning to let them pass through me quickly while it's happening is a true gift that I have yet to conquer completely but I work at it. Only the truly enlightened have that under full control. I am aware that the longer we hang onto unhealthy 'stuff' the more it affects our mental and physical health.

I have dealt with agoraphobia (panic attacks) for years. I was married when they first started. I have practiced the tools I've learned throughout the years to deal with it and control it most days when something stressful shows up. I rarely panic over anything now but can still feel some of the symptoms of anxiety and then physical pain when highly stressed. We do that to ourselves with our overthinking of the worse scenarios possible happening, most of which only ever happens in our minds. Being aware of how I am feeling is the key for me and doing healthy practices daily helps me. Finding humour in the smallest things helps release anxiety.

The fact that I am still writing is very good for stress and good for my memory. It keeps me focused. When the same stresses are ongoing for long periods it can take over and overwhelm us. It is a choice and daily task to stay mentally and physically healthy.

Every morning I have some aches and pains when I first wake up. I walk around a bit stiff at first but the moment I open my blinds I smile. If the sun is out I smile bigger! I look at the sky and then watch the people go by and thank God for another day! I live on a busy street and it makes me feel not as alone. I get to have another day to live and do what I want. I think 'How lucky am I?' on a good day. Something my family that has crossed over does not get to do anymore. I think about that more than ever now and appreciate these small moments.

I do stretches, meditations and energy healings daily that take away the pain from the fibromyalgia. It helps me so much! When I stay in a positive mindset and relax my body enough, I can walk up to two hours a day sometimes. What a blessing to be able to do that considering my health issue and age. In some ways I feel healthier now than five or even ten years ago when I could only walk twenty minutes a day and come home in so much pain. Now I do at least one hour minimum every day and don't have to sit as soon as I get home. I also have to climb 32 steps every day. It has taken a lot of discipline to be well and stay independent. Determination and discipline is the key! It's become a way of life for me that I enjoy.

I know there are older people doing much more that are in incredible shape but unless you have fibromyalgia or live with someone that does people just don't know how debilitating it can be. It is one of many 'invisible diseases.' People see me and have told me I look younger than I am and healthy. It's because I do the work. Doing what we love every day and feeling at peace inside can give us a glow that no drug could ever do. When I am feeling that glow on my walks I feel people are drawn to smile back and say hello. Our energy we give out makes all the difference in how others see us.

There are times I have felt like someone took a baseball bat to my body and beat me with it. That usually only happens now when something comes up in my life that stresses me instantly. Shock to my mind and heart can accelerate pain in my body in a matter of minutes and set off the fibro. I've become much better at handling it.

It is days like today when I can find humour in the not so pretty things about aging. I am standing in front of the mirror naked and wondering wtf happened?! I say this with great humour and with all honesty. It really does suck how our bodies deteriorate in front of our eyes. What are you gonna do? Suck it up and smile because gravity has the final say. We do our best to stay in shape as long as we are able. That's all we can do. If someone wants to get surgery's, botox and whatever else that is available now to avoid aging, good for them. Dying my hair since I was in my mid-forties is the one thing I indulged in that I have yet to stop doing. Other than that I chose a long time ago to accept the process and to stay authentic to the real me as much as possible.

Diane M. Waterman

Who I see looking back at me today is a woman that has sixty five years of wear and tear on her pear-shaped body, stretch marks from carrying her now grown four babies and saggy boobs. I see much softer skin, thick thighs and a pouch belly. I see some roots peeking through from her box dyed hair and I see brand new teeth that she loves and appreciates when they smile back at her. At her last optometrist appointment five years ago she was told she has the beginnings of cataracts. Lovely! She is grateful for it all. She's earned it all!

When I look into her eyes I see acceptance on a good day like today. I see a woman who has been through hell and back many times. She is still standing and loves who she is despite the inevitable dying body. She knows that true beauty comes from the inside and that the shell of a body is temporary but her soul and her true self will get to live on. That alone is beautiful. She has had more blessings than she can count and is deeply grateful for. She loves life and all of its blessings and challenges. On a good and positive day it is easy for her to stay in this mind set.

Despite the aging body I see a loving soul that knows she always needs to work on herself spiritually, mentally and physically to keep her independence for as long as she possibly can. I see tears of appreciation realizing she's made it this far, a privilege her mom and two sisters never had. On this special birthday of becoming a senior I see a survivor of plenty who took huge risks in her life and is still here to share and talk about them to not only help her but others as well. She has learned that being open about her own pain helps others open up and overcome their pain.

She has survived the past ten years of financial stress that should have killed her. I see a woman yearning to still be loved by a partner in crime, because this lady still has more raging hormones than any teenager. *she grins* She still thinks like a forty year old and she has a heart and soul that was made to love. I see a woman that still has many desires and dreams. I see a momma bear that would kill to protect her cubs. I see a fighter who can withstand any storm and I see a child who is sometimes vulnerable like a broken little bird that could barely keep it together from the deep pain of heartbreak and loneliness. I see wisdom, continued growth and a great will to Keep Going. She now looks at her wrinkles and worn out body and smiles with contentment. She made it to her senior years and is very grateful for it all!

It was time to snap out of it and carry these good feelings of appreciation with me all day. I have a doctor's appointment today. I rarely go to the doctor more than once a year for a check-up. I don't take medications of any kind. My blood pressure is great. I do take daily vitamins. I go see my children and grandchildren when I can, I sing when I want, I work on my other passions daily of walking, meditating and writing. I go out and have a lot of fun dancing every weekend with friends. Laughter and fun is so important for me and keeps me going.

All in all I'm doing alright for a newly senior. I know I should maybe slow down a little but I just can't seem to and definitely don't want to. I figure I can do that when my body dies. Sitting or lying around all day long doing nothing would be very hard on my mind and body.

I look through my closet to find something appropriate to wear for my doctor's appointment. I start getting dressed and pick out a colourful, blue flowered sweater to wear and I pull on my black jeans. I sit at my table and look into my ten times magnified mirror *eye roll* to lift the now deepened and saggy eye lids to put on a little eye shadow. The only smooth skin I have now are the bottoms of my feet. *chuckles* I take good care of them as well with doing my own pedicures every two weeks. Staying groomed makes me feel good and even when I am broke I don't need to look it. If you look good on the outside you feel better inside.

I must say my magnified mirror sure helps with the nose hair trimming. Lordy! How the heck did that happen?! Losing hair where I want it and grooming hair that is growing where I don't want it is not fun. It is like a full time job now. Plucking stray thick hairs with tweezers is almost a daily thing for me. Cripes sake!

I remember when the trimming nose hair started happening in my early forties and I talked to my dad about it over the phone one day. He was literally crying because he was laughing so hard on the other end of the phone. I went on about how pissed off I was that I now had to trim nose hairs. A memory I had of him doing this dangerous procedure when I was a young woman was what brought up the subject. Now it was me doing the same. It was one of the many aging things I had to accept with a little complaining and a lot of humour. What else can we do?! The more I went on about it, the more my dad laughed. I love those memories of my dad. It always made me happy to make him laugh that hard. He was making snorkelling sounds as he laughed out loud in a good and hearty belly laugh.

I don't wear much make-up daytime, if any at all, and I find too much of it can age people more. Less is far prettier and cleaner looking in my opinion. A little face makeup, some blush and a touch of mascara and shadow is plenty when I have an appointment to go to. Most times I wear none other than lipstick when I go out walking. I'm so pale I do need a little color.

It's the eye brows that have literally become haywire. *cringe* They certainly took on a mind of their own once I got into my fifties and they have definitely thinned out. I have to trim and pluck what I have left and then try and draw them on to not look too overdone. It's a royal pain and not easy to do. My love for art and drawing helps. I could give up and let it all go to hell but my own vanity and caring for myself just won't let me.

I have plenty of freckles and age spots that don't bother me at all. With all the blemishes, sags, wrinkles, aches and pains, I am determined to take care of what I still have and to appreciate the good things. I can still walk and take care of me. That is huge!

I surely have learned this much, we are what we tell ourselves we are and I try my best to stay young at heart no matter what falls apart on the exterior. Attitude is the key to staying youthful in the heart and soul. Embrace it all, as annoying as some of it may be. Dealing with the annoying little things and the daily pain are certainly distracting from what I would like to be doing with the time it takes to take care of these things but I'll take it over the alternative. Being honest, grateful and graceful in accepting it all is important in keeping good mental and physical health.

On good days I feel like I am the luckiest woman alive! My goal is to have more and more of these kinds of days. I want younger people to be aware of these things too. As scary as some of it may seem, it's not if you stay in a positive mind set. Accept it, embrace it and do it your way. Just remember the most important thing about aging is healing old hurts and how we feel on the inside.

One of my favourite things about being retired and aging is having a routine but no plans. I go to bed around 1am every night and get up around 8 or 9, depending on how I sleep. I get up, do my routine, eat my breakfast and plan my day ahead.

Keep Going

I love not having to rush out the door to go to work every day. As much as I miss the social part of working outside the home, I don't miss the daily pressures of it. Working on my books in the comfort of my home is something I love and am passionate about so it does not feel like work. Do what you love and it will keep you excited to get up in the morning!

Chapter 7

LESSONS OF HUMILITY

I have to look back in these next chapters to help you understand some things I have learned and how it has helped me in more recent years. As always I am sure I will learn even more to share as I write. One thing I know for sure is that I had yet to learn the lesson of the humility of receiving. I have always stayed humble in giving for others. In my mind this is why we are here… to help others while we learn and grow in whatever way we need to. That's what humility has always been in my mind. I had not yet learned to humble myself in asking for financial help when I could no longer work and needed help. This was a hard pill for me to swallow. I have since had many aha moments along my path of 'lessons learned' in this area. I really don't want to write any more about my marriage but I feel I need to in order to teach some of my smart decisions and not so smart decisions that landed me in trouble financially.

Anyone that has been verbally and physically abused understands how hard it is to escape the constant demeaning manipulation that causes us to stay in a toxic environment. So many fears were instilled in me to keep me with my ex-husband until I finally gained my confidence through therapy and found my way out. I didn't fight for or receive any alimony from my ex-husband for the past now twenty eight years that I have lived alone. He refused to pay anything other than minimum child support when I divorced him. He wrote me letters when I left him begging me to come back and stating I was a good wife and mother. Still, he refused to follow the law of paying me any alimony. My lawyer wanted to go after him for more and I said no. The safety of me and my children were all I was worried about. I had built enough confidence in myself by then that there was nothing that would stop me from divorcing him. I also knew him well enough that he would still make my life more of a living hell if he was made to follow the law and support me and our kids any more than he wanted to. I was very aware of the danger I was still in and decided our lives were more important than the alimony that he was flipping out over. He had called me in a rage when he received the divorce papers calling me every name in the book when he saw he would have to pay the minimum alimony which was $300 a month at the time. The average that women were getting back then making the same wages was $1000 a month that I know I could have fought for. I asked my lawyer to drop the alimony payment. My lawyer had to change some things around to do that because by law my ex would have had to pay it. I felt I had to choose my battles wisely.

That money that my ex has saved over these twenty eight years could have helped me indeed but in the end I knew I would have peace of mind in knowing no matter how difficult he tried to make it for me to divorce him and survive without him, just getting his signature alone was enough back in 1997. My peace didn't come without ongoing struggles. In the end I won more than any amount of money he could ever pay me. I had my dignity back. I don't regret that decision but am still not sure if it was the right one. I deserved the support.

I loved the work of being a mom and taking care of my family for those years. I now had to learn to take care of me too and get us out of the toxic environment. That's where in my mind I was failing. To have the courage to do this on my own with no college degree and working for minimum wage was not easy and a big step to take after being brain washed for years I was too stupid to do anything worthwhile in life.

My main goal was to get his signature on the divorce papers and I got it. If someone handed me a million dollars I wouldn't have felt as good as I did in that moment. I did something very brave that was life changing for me and my family. That was enough for me at the time.

Counselling, for me, was the best thing I ever did. I honestly believe everyone should take at least six months of counselling to clear their 'stuff' before getting married or having children. I take the blame for being weak and tolerating what should have ended the first time I was degraded by him. In counselling we have to face ourselves which for me was really hard to do but so worth the work I did for me and my family.

My marriage was certainly not all bad. It had given me my beautiful children and grandchildren and it was an experience I needed to go through to figure out my true value as a human being. For that I am grateful.

What determination I had gained after healing my broken heart, mind and spirit. There were still fears lingering, lots of them! I had to be aware of my surroundings and watch my back for some years after I left. I had to change my locks in my apartment several times. Those years were both scary and wonderful.

After being controlled in everything I did for nearly twenty years while I was a stay at home mom my ex supported us financially. I was content in being a mom and taking care of my family. I got used to being taken care of financially. The bad part was it was used against me constantly in my marriage and also used to keep me there. It was another form of manipulation for him to use against me. I allowed that. He had full control of everything. He often pointed out he paid for it so he had all the say. It's ironic and profound that I had the final say that ended all of that control.

Women need to make their own money, especially as a safety net. I had given up way too much of myself. Thankfully I was wise enough to save enough money for my first month's rent and bills while working at my first job outside the home at KFC the year before I left him. He had suddenly wanted me working outside the home. I wanted to stay home with my children. My ex hounded me so much about it I finally went to work. In the end that job along with the counselling got my foot in the door for freedom. I had worked there a year and I opened a savings account where I could put away a hundred dollars here and there. I only had $900 saved but that was enough to get me out. Looking back now at how all these steps had come together, even the ones I fought, were bringing me to a new life I never dreamed I could have. My new life wouldn't be without struggles but the freedom from the abuse, that had just been a dream for nearly two decades, was finally in my reach and coming true. Not without struggles but well worth every one of them.

I still needed a car so I did borrow a thousand dollars from my sister Mona when I left my ex-husband to buy a cheap car. I promised her I would pay her back monthly and I did. She was paid back in full after 10 months. It took everything in me to ask her for the loan but I knew I really needed a car. My ex had taken both vehicles when he moved out. It was not just for me but for my kids and so I sucked up my pride that one time and asked Mona for the loan. My sister was working at the time and kindly loaned me the money. It was the first time I ever asked my family for anything. It was a big struggle for me to ask. After having everything I had and did be controlled by someone else for so long it felt like I was suddenly given wings to fly on my own. I was buying my first very own car that was rusty around the bottom but had command start! It was exhilarating! That old Toyota lasted me five years.

The minimum child support for each of my two girls barely covered my children's needs and part of the rent. I had to squeeze every penny together to also pay back that $100 a month to my sister out of the money I was now getting from my new part-time job working for People's Jewelers. Many times I was down to my last five dollars before pay day again. Somehow I paid all my bills and made it all work. The freedom from all the negativity I had lived with for nearly two decades was worth the new struggles I was having. I was happy! After eight months I got hired on full time at my job at the jewelry store and doubled my pay to $500 every two weeks. I was still far from rich but life was good back then!

Money was something I never had to worry about while I was working for fifteen years after that. Me and my children never wanted for anything. Even after my two girls moved out within six years and I lost the minimum child support, I still did well and flourished. As the years went by when I had extra money I loved helping people that had less than I did. I also saved some money as the years went by. It seemed the more I helped others and felt the joy of that feeling, the more money started to fall out of the sky for me as I became happier and happier in my life. It was the law of the universe working with me. Light brings light!

I was living out my passions more and more. It was something I never expected or experienced before. This was happening when I was at the height of my happiness so it makes sense to me now as to why money suddenly flowed to me so easily. I felt euphoric back then. The bliss I felt inside was real! When you are living in bliss and helping others, it is sure to flow back to you freely. It was something new I was learning about and it took me awhile to realize the connection. The law of attraction was working in my favour. I helped anyone that needed it and anyone that didn't because it just felt so good. I got so much more back that money could never buy. The expressions of love and true appreciation from people made me feel good too. It was all so amazing and worth it and without even realizing it was also helping me build my own self-esteem even more along the way. Putting a smile on someone else's face is still my favourite thing to do in life.

I had not felt that kind of bliss, just glimpses of it, for some years after that wonderful time frame because I went to a dark place of great worry when I was suddenly dealing with my sons drug addiction in 2010 and 2011. Those years were very draining mentally, physically and financially. I had pretty much cleared out my bank account trying to help my son. After many dark times and battles, my son thankfully started to recover. Just after all of that stress in 2012 my sister Mona, who was in a very dark place after a divorce, decided to move in with me in Edmonton. We managed to get her a place of her own in the apartment building I was renting in a month later. Within a year she had developed lung cancer. I took on helping to care for her. It was another very dark time. Being around her depressed and sometimes angry energy was very draining for me. She was dealing with a lot. The extra stress elevated my anxiety and in turn activated my fibromyalgia pain constantly. My taking on that energy was not anyone's fault but my own.

All that darkness those struggles created around me in turn activated one struggle after another for the next ten years for me. Without a doubt negative brings more negative. I am not blaming my family for anything, bad things happen in life for everyone. I am blaming me because I didn't handle it the way I should have. No one causes us to worry and get ill but ourselves and I was in constant worry at those times in my life. It is the human part of us and our egos that tend to react to our surroundings. We choose and control how we react.

I worked hard to stay on top of everything in a positive manner but the dark times were very hard to manage when I was surrounded in daily negativity. I could have walked away and turned my back from it all right away but that's not me. I would have worried more if I wasn't there to try and help my family. I did my best to control my over thinking and worrying. That state of mind manifests nothing good for sure and it took me years to pull out of the aftermath of it all.

I loved my sister and love my son so I have no regrets. It was a lot of learning and suffering they went through and I chose to go through it with them learning about many new things I had never dealt with before.

After fifteen years of many blissful times while I worked to then be thrown into the next ten years of so much darkness around me was going to teach me one hard lesson after another.

In 2011 my pain had been so bad I finally had gone to a specialist who diagnosed me with fibromyalgia. I had to quit my job because I could hardly get out of bed some days. I was constantly riddled with pain at the time.

On my worst days of worrying I feared my son might have died when I didn't hear from him for days at a time. I lived in a busy part of Edmonton and the sirens from ambulances could be heard all day and night. It was a scary time as I let my mind make up stories of the worst things possible happening to him. Keeping my thoughts under control so I didn't have a nervous breakdown was a daily job. Again, that was on me.

On top of that there was the burden of surviving financially without a job. I was thankful for the unemployment checks I received after I had quit work but they would run out in a matter of months.

Not being able to work anymore added more worry and

stress for years to come. I was turned down for disability. The government still didn't take fibromyalgia seriously. The grief of missing my job was harder emotionally than I had thought it would be. For fifteen years I thrived at work and I made a lot of friends that I loved. When you leave you leave many friends as well. A few close friends I still keep in touch with. The social part of the job in meeting new people every day was something I was passionate about and would miss daily. My job was fun for me and no matter which store I worked at I always tried to make the atmosphere fun for everyone. I really loved the people and I felt loved in return. It was a lot to have to give up but the mental and physical pain I was in by then was simply unbearable most days. At the time I had not yet connected the emotional pain and worry to the physical pain I was in daily.

Months before I had quit my job I felt I was on a crazy train and saw no way off. Over that two year period I had also used up my savings trying to save my son who had made many suicide attempts by then. I learned many hard lessons in that time. Number one to not dish out my savings to try and save my son who I learned in time had to do it himself. With experience and learning I finally stopped enabling him, told him he wasn't living with me again and he had no choice but to go to detox and sober living. He did both for two years. I stuck by my son through it all as he went into his recovery and healing. Thankfully he is alive and well today and helps others who suffer. I'm really proud of him.

Diane M. Waterman

We get sucked into the hole of doom and gloom and when its close family that needs help it is very hard to pull away and turn your back on them. Those dark years took work to just survive much less live in any kind of bliss. Somehow we all survived it as my son got onto a healthier path. I am so grateful for that. Not all families are so lucky. I feel deeply for those who lose family members through addiction. Just know you did your very best.

To go from being the giver to taking care of number one first was still a continuing learning process for me. I was starting to wake up to it more and more over those years but still had a long way to go in asking for help for myself because by then I was struggling in many areas. I did all I could do as a mother and learned a hard lesson of leaving myself broke trying to help my son who was not ready to help himself, was only harming both of us. That time period was a real eye opener for me of how quickly our lives can change and how much we can survive. It also humbled me even more in knowing none of us are above hard times.

Life carried on and shortly after the drama of my son being ill is when my sister needed me. I stuck by her side until her very last breath. She was in a dark place and it was another very hard time in our lives but the fight to stick it out in the end was so worth it to me and I know for her as well. She fought to live until the bitter end. I keep the happier memories of

Keep Going

our childhood and the many years of us raising our families together close to my heart.

Those years drained me financially, emotionally and physically. The effects it all left on me took hard work and a long time to get well again because I had not made myself a priority too. I vowed to keep going!

Chapter 8

GOD WORKS IN MYSTERIOUS WAYS

On December 30th 2015, my apartment was broken into when I was out one evening with friends. The full story is in my book, *You Have to Go Now*. I won't go into too many details other than it was a nightmare! Not only were my beautiful jewelry and some family heirlooms stolen but my sister Donna's ashes that I had in a little heart can were stolen as well. I had kept them in a pewter jewelry box on my dresser that had been a gift I had given her many years before with her name engraved on it. It was a devastating night for me with her ashes being stolen, never mind everything else. Some of my mom and sisters jewelry was mixed amongst my own that the robbers had taken without any thought or care. Most importantly I lost my sense of security in my own home for some time to come.

The positive from the break in, if there could be any, was I got paid out from my insurance company enough money to pay for a headstone for my parents and to help get me through the next ten months of putting food on my table and keeping the lights on.

I didn't get half of what my loss was worth and I had to live with that. The value of my sister's ashes was priceless. No amount of money could make up for that loss. Many times something terrible happens to us for reasons that help us in the end. It's hard to imagine that when we are in it and heartbroken but I am learning this to be true more and more. I never in my wildest dreams thought that my home would ever be broken into or that these financial problems I struggled with in my later years would ever happen to me. It felt like there was just one bad thing after another happening during those years. I was still healing from the loss of my sister and dealing with my financial struggles. Being robbed was certainly the last thing I needed. If we could only see the long term outcome from what we see instantly as nightmares, maybe we wouldn't go into the full blown stresses and the pain of the hard experiences so quickly? We'd just let them pass, feeling what we need to feel in that moment without worry, knowing it is another test to make us stronger and wiser in the end. The older I get the more I am finding that seems to be the answer to my many questions, in many cases if not all, in our journey here. I only wish it were that easy to get through. For some it is.

When we take time to look back we often see a different and more positive perspective. Just like what happened in seeing me as a child standing alone in my grandmother's kitchen has now taken on a whole new perspective for me. That is what healing, maturity, wisdom and growth does for us.

My father passed away 34 days after my apartment was robbed. More despair! It was yet another devastating heartbreak. Grief is something I feel we do have to feel and go through to not get stuck in unhealed pain. The past ten years had brought one difficult trial after another it seemed. All I could do was deal with one thing at a time, one day at a time and so I grieved for my dad who I loved dearly. His loss was one of many by then and my family circle just kept getting smaller and smaller.

My laptop had been stolen as well during the robbery with the 22 chapters I had already written for my book *You Have to Go Now*. Thankfully I found the USB stick I had been using and retrieved the book while having to purchase another laptop to finish the project. I couldn't give up on that book. It was so healing for me to write. I decided to invest some of the insurance money and publish *You Have to Go Now*. It was another risk I took to also help others and at least try and make a living from doing something I love and feel passionate about. Writing gave me a reason to get up each morning and to heal from the mental and physical effects I was still going through at that time. Following our passions is the most important thing we can do for ourselves. It brings us good karma. In the end writing about my grief in losing family members, my best friend and so much more around that time did help me a great deal. I feel it saved me from going down a much darker road.

By October of 2016 the insurance money had ran out. I was now at a point financially I might soon have to finally suck it up and actually ask for social assistance to help me. Something I had been avoiding at all costs. I wished I could have stayed working but I knew in dealing with the fibromyalgia I couldn't physically do it anymore at that time. I lived with physical pain day and night. The break in and losing my dad had really triggered it again and it was daily work for me to do what I could mentally and physically to try and ease the pain and to Keep Going.

I was still not free of my money problems which piled on even more stress. I didn't know where to turn some days and was definitely not in the right mindset to turn things around. I felt I was too old for anyone to hire me by this point which I found to be true when I did apply for part time work later on. It was a strange place to be after being sought after by managers in previous years to work for them. I prayed often and I knew deep down I was learning an important lesson in humility and it was taking its own sweet time coming. Having to go to ask for financial help was a very difficult place to be in my life. I told myself to think positive and that it would only be temporary every day. I would survive the internal shame somehow. After all I had become aware by then that courage and strength was all I needed. I could do this too. I had placed the shame on myself, no one else did. I had to let that go. My pride was taking a big hit and I had to accept that bad things can happen to anyone and I was no exception to that rule. I was being humbled in a whole new light.

I was surrounded by struggles constantly for those years and I couldn't find a way out of it to get back on my feet and feel happy in my life again. I had moments but not enough to stay in my faith and to stay positive as a rule day in and day out. The survival mode seemed to be constantly on. Being negative was something I tried being aware of. I know I had far too many moments of self-doubt and worry. I would sometimes get angry as well because I had witnessed so much deceit from others because of addictions in taking advantage of family, including me. Many days I struggled to rise above it all. It was a lot to deal with and I felt I had every right to be angry but in the end the anger only brought me down further into the depths of darkness.

The financial worry was a constant dark cloud that I had yet to conquer. I was still meditating and doing what I could in my daily practices to survive but I was still not in a good head and heart space because I still had some of the darkness of those past years hanging onto me. I was still working at letting it all go.

My first two books were getting great reviews and I had made enough to pay for what it cost me to publish them but no miracles. It certainly was not going to pay my monthly bills. That's not why I write but I certainly wouldn't turn down a miracle in that department either. Having the money to market even one of them would have been great but that opportunity had yet to arise. Social media had been the only way to promote them for now. Finding a job outside the home was out at that time. I had trouble even typing some days because my fingers hurt but I wouldn't quit and was at least writing. I was doing the best I could while keeping my faith on the good days. Real wisdom and faith is to let go of that control we think we have that causes worry and just follow God's path. I had to do what I could control and to leave the rest to God.

I could move money around on my credit cards but using it for rent as well meant I would run them up so fast that it would hurt me more in the long run. I had to think everything through before I did anything. My line of credit and charge card would keep me going for a while but I knew I couldn't keep it up for long without getting in over my head fast. So, it was time to suck up my pride. Social assistance was the next step for now. At least they might help pay my rent. That would help a lot to release some of the constant stress I was under.

My heart tightened at the thought of it. God forbid I couldn't pay on my credit cards! I was the 'responsible one' according to my dad and I did my best to always be that way for me as well. I was very prideful that way. My excellent credit score all my life was very important to me. Oh the expectations we put on ourselves!

Looking back at that time I still had four years until I would get my full pension at 65 and I was scared to death I couldn't make it! "This too will pass." I repeated time and time again whenever my stress level was at a high as that dark cloud kept following me around day after day. Just saying those words gave me some brief relief because I knew it was true. The hard times always do pass. It's when there's one after another that really, really test our faith.

What we don't realize in these hard times is that these are some of the greatest blessings of learning that are bestowed upon us. When our faith is tested it is a true life lesson. 'How lucky am I that I have somewhere to turn in my hard times,' is how I should have been thinking about going for assistance, not wallowing in the shame of asking for help. Again, perception is everything.

It is now my opinion that floating through life without a challenge teaches us absolutely nothing. The good part is in the end we see the true value of each lesson. Some lessons takes years to learn. Some of us are indeed hard headed. *grin* The main thing is to make it through and to see each lesson for what it truly is…a gift. We often have to lose in life in order to gain knowledge.

Keep Going

Giving into darkness and giving up would have been oh so easy, so easy. At times when it felt too hard to go on I fought back quickly with light and positive thoughts and routines because I had experienced deep depression before and never wanted to go there again. It had caused my anxiety disorder 'agoraphobia' to get far worse by letting myself go too long into depression and staying in bed for three days in the year 2000.

At that time I had no clue of the effect it would have on me. I learned a lot since then to never let myself go there for that long again. As happy as I was at that time, I had gone through so much loneliness from being without any physical touch from a man for 3 years after my divorce. I had finally met someone I fell for, but it didn't go anywhere. We had an argument over the phone and I was heartbroken. I had felt at the time that he was the one for me. I was wrong. We remained friends for years but nothing more. I believe now my connection to him was to meet his sister who became a close friend and I loved dearly.

I never go to bed anymore and just stay there when I go through struggles with heartbreak and sadness no matter how tough it is. I know many people suffer with clinical depression. If you are reading this I am proud of you because you are still here fighting. The sadness and heartbreak kind of depression I've experienced is by happenstance, not clinical depression which from what I have read and learned is far worse. God bless those who struggle. I can only imagine your pain.

Diane M. Waterman

I have always felt like God had my back and I say that often. My faith has been tested for sure in these past years. There were times I had brief doubt and wondered if He was listening at all but not for long. Prayer helped me pull through many hard days. I asked God many times what lessons was I supposed to be learning going through these struggles in more recent years. Giving to others was so easy for me, but to take, not so much. I was still on the path of figuring out why?!

I do take a lot of pride in staying independent but sometimes we can be too independent and I was just starting to figure out why I was so stubborn in receiving help from anyone. Part of it for me was because of the control I was under in my marriage. I had been controlled by fear and money for so long I wanted to be completely independent and never have to rely on anyone ever again to support me financially. I now feel there in lay the reason why I became more stubborn in taking anything from anyone or asking for help in the future. It had been used to manipulate me for nearly two decades. That experience made me feel bad about myself for so long I had made up my mind I would never take anything ever again from anyone. I would never allow myself to be vulnerable that way again in giving up my independence. That along with always being a giver my whole life made it a struggle for me to ask anyone for help in my time of need.

At this point I just wanted to learn more, and I believe as I continue to write, I will. It's a wonderful tool with which I have been blessed.

It's funny how when we mention some things the Universe automatically sends us the answer we are looking for when we pay attention. There is no doubt in my mind I am being guided when I write. It just came to me in this very moment that asking for help is really a true source of 'strength and courage.' AHA! And there it is! For me it would take way more strength and courage to ask for help when I need it than to not ask. I had to dig deeper for that courage and to get over myself! An amazing moment of clarity for me!

I was always way too hard on myself believing others expect the same from me as I do. That's not the way life works. It is okay NOT to be perfect and to ask for help. It has nothing to do with making mistakes or being flawed. It's just getting through life's hard times and a part of surviving. It's okay to drop the mask to be humble and vulnerable. It's okay! If I can find it in my heart to do for others without judgement why not have that same compassion for me too?! God wants us to be vulnerable and I am worthy of compassion. I certainly would never take advantage of anyone. He knows my heart.

Was I still feeling remnants of unworthiness from my past? That was sad for me to think after all I had survived and healed in the years during and after my divorce but the learning never really ends…

Tears are falling as I write this because I am letting this truth sink in at this moment. 'Humility' and being vulnerable in our times of need is a source of true strength in character, not a weakness as I had always viewed it because of my own past and my strong need to be independent. I had viewed giving up my independence in any way as being weak. By the end of this chapter I have learned a valuable lesson. I now get to pass that lesson onto you with so much love and new found humility in my heart. Receiving with grace and humility is a true source of strength and courage. Putting it into practice would still not be easy but at least now I was more aware.

Everything I went through and the decisions from my past had led me to this moment. Was it a wrong choice to not push my ex-husband to pay me what I surely deserved? Was it a wrong choice to clean out my savings when my son wasn't well and I was trying everything I could to desperately save his life? Only to learn over time I was doing the worse thing possible by enabling him. Was it wrong to get wrapped up in worry that added to my poor health while trying to take care of my family? In this moment I would say no. I needed those steps in order to learn the lesson of humility for my own self-care and feeling worthy. Would I do the same things now if the same situations arose today as they occurred back then? Probably not because I am not the same person I was even five years ago. Every decision I made back then was fear based. I would like to believe I would handle some things differently now.

Keep Going

Even after all the work I had put in I had certainly grown but I still wasn't there yet. I would need even more financial lessons yet before I would finally get the full lesson of being humble in receiving and feeling worthy of it. God wasn't done with me yet but I was slowly beginning to understand more that it's okay to sometimes put me and my needs first and that all the worry and stress I go through is simply brought on by my own thoughts. Controlling that is another story.

Thank you God for each lesson I have learned.

Chapter 9

NEAR BOTTOM

My pride was taking a HUGE hit when I was standing in line at Alberta Works in October 2017. This was what my world had come to six years after not being able to go back to work. I managed to hang on for those six years but now I was strapped for money and down to my credit card and line of credit. I had made the final decision to reach out for help and it was excruciating for me. I was experiencing utter and complete shame of the worse kind. I was learning about HUMILITY in a whole different light. That shame was self-inflicted of course. At least I wasn't living on the street, yet. There is always something to be thankful for in the worse situations but I saw none on this day as I stood boldly in my ego. I was feeling sorry for myself. I had to believe this was only temporary. I was still learning the real positives of this kind of humility. There is nothing I love more than experiencing making a difference in the lives of others but to ask for help myself, well, all I can say is I was getting a good dose of reality and how that feels. Only hitting bottom can bring you to this place and this felt darn close for me. I had yet to see the light in the experience.

I felt my heart squeezing tight. My eyes were teary. Self-pity was something I hated but on this particular day I was past caring. I had to suck it up and ask for help to pay my rent. This was something unimaginable for me. Killing me was not an option. "I can do this!" I told myself over and over. It was either swallow my pride or live on the street?! My choice! There was no way I was living with my grown children. The choice was mine and mine alone. Street or welfare? How many bad decisions had I made to end up here? Blaming me was easy when in all reality this was due to my health issues and some of my choices on my path to grow more. It's easier to see it more clearly with experience and when looking back. Not so much when you're in the thick of it.

"God help me!" I whispered.

I have a real compassion for the homeless. I treat them with the utmost respect, always have. I know there are many homeless out there who see hard times and most are not addicts as many people believe. Even the addicts deserve a chance to turn their life around. Many do. Many people have exhausted all other options because of health issues, losing jobs or other issues. I have never passed judgement on the homeless and in that moment I was sure glad I didn't because I was one step away from it. I had talked to many homeless people who were barely surviving on $800 a month while trying to get back on their feet.

It was my turn in line so I stepped up and gave my name to the receptionist at the counter and then took a seat. I couldn't get the worry and self-inflicted shame out of my head. My overthinking ego was having a field day. When my name was called I went inside a booth and sat in front of a lovely lady with long blond hair. She asked me why I was there. I took a deep breath and started telling her my situation. She was typing everything I told her on her computer. Sixty one years old and it had come to this in my life?! I felt like I was asking for a hand out and that the world would judge me. I was already judging myself big time! I now knew how so many others must have felt going through this process.

The lady asked me a lot of questions. I answered each one honestly and then she asked me if I had any family. Suddenly I couldn't speak and I felt tremendous pain in my heart. I thought, 'Oh no, I'm going to cry!' Even writing this now I still feel the pain as I did that day. That's the one topic that will get me every time, 'family.'

She passed me a tissue and I tried to speak as the silent tears fell but I couldn't get a word out. My dad had passed just nine months before and this brought up the sadness of losing him as well. I slowly got out that my mother and father and my two sisters had passed. "I have two siblings left but rarely hear from them. They both deal with bad addictions." I whispered. At the time, that was my family. Gone, all gone just like that! My children were not in the place to help me and I was not going to ask them for help. In my mind I was supposed to take care of them, not the other way around.

I had to do this as humiliating as it was. I felt like I was down at the bottom of the barrel and I was drowning right then and there in a huge puddle of grief, shame and self-pity. It was going to take all the training I had learned to get me through this. I had to be grateful to have these people to turn to but I just couldn't see it in that moment. I wiped away the tears as the kind lady kept typing on her computer.

The lady was so compassionate towards me. She approved me for the assistance and because I was already getting my CCP at $320 a month that had started on my 60th birthday, they could give me another $500. It was a huge relief!! Along with my CPP it was at least enough to cover my rent of $700 a month. I could use my credit cards for food, to keep my lights on and to pay for other necessities for a while. Back then I was trying very hard not to have to give up my car, at least not until I had no choice. I needed it to still get around. I couldn't walk more than twenty minutes anywhere at that time. To walk to get groceries back then was out of the question.

Having to go down this road didn't help my self-esteem for sure but the relief of worrying about paying my rent every month would hopefully relieve some of the daily stress I was under. Even though it was some relief I still worried for the future. I could only move money around on my credit to keep the lights on for so long. Then what? Sell my car and then what? The worry and negative stories I made up in my mind were relentless some days. Thankfully I was aware enough to catch them and turn it around as much as possible telling myself I could handle whatever was thrown at me. I worked hard to not overthink and go down the rabbit hole of darkness. I had made the scary steps, got through what I had feared and I was okay and grateful. Feeling fear and stepping through it is the most life changing growth we can do.

I wrote in my grateful book every morning 5 things I was grateful for. I could always find something to be grateful for, even waking up each day. My thoughts were key and the more negative thoughts I had about being on welfare without a doubt the more shame and guilt I would feel which would only make me ill. And God forbid people found out I was having these struggles! What would everyone think of me?! Only my closest two friends and a few family members knew. That would have been more shame that only I would place on me. And here I am four years later telling the world? Now that is growth!

In all reality what people think of me is none of my business. I know this kind of worry had only come to me because of the nasty comments I have heard from people over the years that hate on the homeless and people receiving welfare that are barely surviving. Do some abuse the system? Without a doubt, but most of the homeless I have met are compassionate and kind human beings with a big heart that are simply down on their luck. We can all learn from them as I have.

I was not yet seeing this new kind of humility in a good way but I was getting there. The fact that I had found the courage to ask for help which was really a blessing in that moment, was still blind to me. I see it now big time! At that time I had only let myself feel the shameful and painful side because of my ego. This would take a while to process and that is okay. I was still learning…

I kept telling myself things would get better and easier, yet with all the sadness and worry I had been going through in those years how could I really believe what I was telling myself daily?! At least the pushing myself part of it and practicing daily routines kept me alive and hopeful. I did feel grateful that I'd at least made the steps and made it through the process of asking for help, which in my mind was the hardest part.

I had also started to learn around this time I should have been staying in the grateful mode while praying rather than constantly asking God for more help. I changed my prayers to grateful prayers. Asking for help constantly is annoying to God, I am sure, because to keep praying for the same things over and over means I am not in my faith. I did my best to be grateful for the little things and to find as many moments

Diane M. Waterman

of happiness in the times I got to spend with my kids and grandkids and in working daily on my passions. I would follow my passions as an artist and whatever brought me joy in the moment. Just getting a hug from my grandkids or picking up my guitar to sing a song always made my days a little brighter. I worked hard to focus on what mattered the most.

I had stepped through my fears and asked social assistance for help. I survived the stories of shame my own thoughts had brought onto me. The extra money had somewhat eased my worries and stress level at the time. Living in gratitude is so important and I was very grateful for the extra help. I had found my courage to finally ask for help. I believe staying in the fight with courage and a grateful heart in the end is what got me through it.

Keep Going...

Chapter 10

TIME FOR CHANGE

I had put my back out while I was shovelling snow one day in the winter of 2018. I felt the click in my lower back as I was gently pushing the shovel. That's all it took. I carefully made my way up the stairs to the third floor to my apartment. It only got worse after that. I had put my back out many times in previous years but not as often since I started doing yoga. This time I was a few years older than the last time it had happened. With age it seemed to be more painful and took longer to heal. It was a full week of torture! Getting up to go to the bathroom, never mind trying to cook with my body bent over, was just awful! Life was a living hell that week! Anyone that has suffered putting their back out will understand this. I had to lean on the counter to keep myself partly upright enough to cook. I tried gentle yoga to help it but nothing worked. I just had to let my body go through its course of healing. I don't take medications because I am sensitive to most and I am leery of side effects.

I distinctly remember feeling so exhausted from trying to get around on day four that just walking from my bathroom to my chair in the living room, which was no more than ten steps away, was too much for me! I really felt like giving up! Between the scariness of being alone when I wasn't well and the suffering from the excruciating back pain, I knew if I died in that moment I wouldn't mind one bit. The pain was tortuous every time I moved an inch! If I could just go to sleep and it would be all over I would have been just fine with it. I don't believe I had ever felt so ready to give up in my entire life as I did in that moment.

I love life so much but sometimes it has been beyond hard. For someone that worked hard to stay positive this was where I was at that moment in time. I'm being completely honest. I questioned how much fight is one person supposed to have in them?! I was heartbroken that everything was so hard and that I felt so very alone. Thankfully, I am a fighter and I also despise self-pity so I never stay in it for long. "Keep going! Tomorrow will be a little better!" I cried as I took a deep breath and pushed myself to slowly continue the steps to my chair.

I had to push myself hard through each day and that particular day I had to push extra hard. It was a full week before I could almost stand upright, still with some pain and tightness but an improvement. Thankfully I could see a little light again and bring myself out of the deep darkness.

It was in this time of suffering that I told myself I was not going to spend another winter in Edmonton. I promised myself that. I was going to take care of number one. I really felt I wouldn't survive another winter there. I needed to make a change for survival sake and I knew I had to do it, again, on my own.

Many times I felt completely alone there. I never felt like it was home to me, even with my kids living there. They had all moved to Edmonton about five years after I did. I did what I could to help them out while I was working and we had many happy times together there but I moved there in 2004 because it was necessary, not because I wanted to. My rent had doubled in six months in Fort McMurray when the boom happened and as a single mom working in retail I was forced to leave. I never liked the big city life. The atmosphere is completely different than in smaller towns. I met a lot of wonderful people who I love but my time there was up. I felt it in my heart, body and soul. Too much had changed with me not being able to work anymore and with the loss of my family and two close friends by then, I was about as low as I'd ever been that week. With so many losses and nobody left to talk to going through that very tough week really opened my eyes. I realized how quickly my life could end too. I wanted to make the best of whatever time I have left here. I certainly had not been living my best life and I felt it was only getting worse.

My kids are adults and had their own lives to live. I never want to be a burden for them or anyone else. There were times they helped out when they could and I always appreciated it. I saw my son often when we would go to church together but even that stopped that winter and we saw each other much less. My two girls had moved to the west end a half hour away from where I was living. I was always aware of that and didn't want them driving on the busy streets to my place maybe feeling they needed to take care of me, especially in winter time.

I was desperate by then to get out the slump I had been in for too many years. I felt a change for me as a positive move for not only me but for them as well. I know my kids want me to be happy.

The loneliness of the past winters in Edmonton had only grown darker for me. Winter time is hard for many people. Sometimes a big change is necessary for survival. Life can take us in a new direction unexpectedly to hopefully help us find some kind of happiness again if we are in a slump.

Two years before, in September 2016, an ole friend of mine that I had not seen for many years was in Edmonton when I went out to celebrate my 60th birthday. It's amazing how things happen to bring you what you need sometimes. I don't believe in coincidences and it was a complete surprise when she showed up at my birthday celebration.

Dinah who still lived in Fort McMurray was in Edmonton visiting with friends and family. I was thrilled to see her again when she walked into the New West club where I had been celebrating. We had a great time together and vowed we would see each other again soon.

It took almost three more years until I ended up seeing Dinah again in Edmonton July of 2019, just after the worst winter I had ever spent there with the back incident. The timing was perfect! I still wanted to move but had not yet figured out a way to do it. Being broke was still a problem I had to somehow figure out and work around. I knew once my mind was made up nothing would stop me.

We went out to see some friends who were playing at the Legion that weekend. Going out never cost me anything because I always drank water for many years. I was happy just to get out, dance a little and socialize. Being with Dinah again felt like old times of when we used to go out together in Fort McMurray before I moved away. Being with her and having fun made me miss Fort McMurray even more. I just didn't know how I could ever make it work to move back there again. I didn't know where the money would come from but the wheels were certainly spinning and I knew in my heart that Fort McMurray was where I wanted to go. It was the closest I felt to home having raised my children there with my sisters and their families and it was close enough that my kids and I could still visit whenever we wanted to.

I felt God had sent me a friend I really needed at the time. I saw it as an opportunity to try and find some kind of happiness again. I had felt my spirit and body were slowly dying that past winter and I needed to make a change. So much had already changed in my life. My closest friend in Edmonton Beverly had passed away in 2010. I missed her every day and being off work since 2011 I was still missing that part of my social life as well. I longed to be around people again. My favourite dance club the New West had closed down in 2018. I missed going to dances and seeing friends. My friend Verna had passed away as well. She was my favourite person to dance with. She was so full of life and love. I missed her terribly. No longer having that outlet to look forward to was hard for me. I am someone who needs to be social.

When Dinah came back in my life I felt the opportunity for some kind of happiness again was knocking at my door. She is younger than I am by 21 years but she is an old soul and I am very young at heart. We are very much alike when it comes to our hearts. I know there is nothing either of us wouldn't do for each other. Before Dinah left I had promised I would try and go to Fort McMurray for a weekend in the future to visit her and to see how I felt going back there. I had no clue how I would make it happen but when I make a promise I tend to keep it.

My sisters and our families had moved to Fort McMurray in 1978. In 2004, being a single mom by then, I could no longer afford the rent that had suddenly sky rocketed. I had no choice but to move away from my family and friends. It had been a scary and a big move to make on my own to St. Albert first and then to Edmonton the following year. The company I was working for at the time set me up to work at their store in St. Albert right after the move. It was a matter of survival back then.

Fifteen years later I had become even braver when it came to taking risks. Rent prices in Fort McMurray had dropped since I had left and I believed if this was meant to be it would work out. I do believe in fate. Dinah had showed up in my life again for a reason and I believe it was to give me the encouragement that I needed to make a change at a time when I was desperate for change.

In August of 2019 I decided to finally go to Fort McMurray for a visit. I knew it would be hard going back there with my sisters not there anymore and most of our friends had moved away or passed on. I had not been back to visit for eight years. I also knew I would have to risk using my credit to get me there on the bus. It was just for a weekend and I felt it was a matter of life and death for me to take the risk, so I went.

It was very emotional for me at first entering back into Fort McMurray on the bus. The memories of living there came flooding back of my sisters and our many years of family times together. My heart tightened and it made me miss them so much. I wiped the tears away and told myself "this will be good for me." I knew within minutes after I stepped off the bus that I had to move back. Other than moving back to Newfoundland, which would have been too far away from my kids and grandkids, this was the closest I felt to home. I didn't know for certain how I was going to make it happen because I was still broke and living off my meagre monthly checks and credit, but my mind was made up.

If I moved downtown I could drive to get anything I needed in five minutes. Being an anxious driver in Edmonton this would be far better for me and I definitely felt I wouldn't feel as isolated.

The price of housing had dropped in Fort McMurray from when I had lived there and my confidence was up that just maybe I could make it happen. Even though I was barely getting by I knew with my faith feeling strong again and with my determination I would somehow get a miracle that would help me make it happen.

I had so much fun when I was there for that visit I didn't want to leave to go back to Edmonton. The whole atmosphere felt more like home. The warmth and friendliness I felt from strangers reminded me of going home to Newfoundland. There are so many people from the east coast living in Fort McMurray. I felt more relaxed and I was smiling all the time. I stayed with friends Ron and Mona who were sweethearts and treated me

Keep Going

like gold. I didn't want to burden Dinah by staying with her because I knew she had her kids to take care of but we did go out together and she took me around to see some of the town again. After a fun filled weekend I reluctantly went back to Edmonton knowing this was not going to be easy but if I was going to make a move it had to be before winter.

It took me about a week before I made the final decision that I was going to do everything I could to make the move happen. Leaving my children would not be easy for any of us and it was clear they didn't want me to move. I felt I had no choice and really worried they might resent the move, after all they had all followed me to Edmonton. I had to stay for them or be selfish for once and consider my own happiness. The common sense thing to do was to take care of me. I was no good to myself or them if I was unhappy and depressed.

I wasn't getting any younger and time was ticking. I had to do what was best for me and my mental health. I had not been truly happy since I had to quit my job in 2011. I had loved life so much and enjoyed spoiling my family when I was working but so much had changed for me. I had already gone through so many life changing events solo and survived, I knew with God's help I could do this too.

September 1st, 2019, I put my notice into the owner of my building that I was going to be moving to Fort McMurray.

He was not happy about it. I had lived in that building for fourteen years. He said they hated to see me go but understood I needed a change.

Next I went online to find a place to rent in Fort McMurray. To my surprise the rent was still much higher there than in Edmonton. I had gotten a good deal on the apartment I was in for the past years because the owners were reasonable and only raised the rent by fifty dollars twice in the fourteen years I lived there. Now to find another place in Fort McMurray for $700 a month wasn't looking good. The more I searched the more I could already see this was not going to be an easy feat. Most one bedroom places I found were $1000 or more. You could get a basement 'bedroom' for $700 a month. No way did I want to live in a basement confined to a bedroom. I know I need as much light as possible coming in wherever I live. I kept looking daily for three weeks straight. My eyes were sore from staring at the computer screen searching for that perfect place. I had lucked out once in my apartment in Edmonton, could I be that lucky twice? It wasn't looking good but I wouldn't give up!

I did a post on one of the Fort McMurray sites looking for help and asking why it was still so much more expensive to rent there than in Edmonton? I knew there were many more vacancies in Fort McMurray since the 2016 fire. Thousands did not move back after that devastating fire. One woman commented on my post that I would never find an apartment in Fort McMurray for $700 a month and that I was dreaming. I replied, "Thank you but you don't know me very well. I have a lot of Faith."

In the meantime I was already packing, determined to make it happen. I had also left my phone number on a couple of answering machines of places to rent but no one was getting back to me yet. I called low income housing and they had a long waiting list up to two years. "Keep the faith." I whispered time and time again. Then one day after three weeks of frustration I decided to stop looking and to rely completely on my faith alone. I felt in that moment if it was meant to be it would come to me. I closed my laptop and I led back in my lazy boy to meditate. I needed to relax and to give my burning eyes a break. Ten minutes into the meditation my phone rang. I opened my eyes, picked up my phone and said, "hello."

A man's voice spoke. "Hello. Is this Diane?"

"Yes it is." I replied.

"You left a message on my phone asking about our apartments? My name is Carl."

"Yes I did." I replied as I sat straight up in my chair.

Carl was such a nice man. We hit it off right away. We found out we knew some of the same people in Fort McMurray. Carl is a spiritual and kind man. He asked me why I had left

Fort McMurray fifteen years earlier. I explained how I had no choice back in 2004 because my rent had doubled in six months. I was a single mom and worked in retail at the time. I just couldn't afford it so I had to move away. He was very understanding and compassionate.

The only problem was he was asking $1300 a month for a one bedroom; almost double what I was paying in Edmonton for a two bedroom. The buildings were about the same age. I explained to him I was on social assistance then and just couldn't do it. My heart dropped but I still had a good feeling about this man and continued to keep my faith. Carl said he would talk to his parents who were the owners of the building as well and he would get back to me. When I hung up I knew even if he gave me a deal of $1000 a month I still couldn't pay that much but somewhere deep down I felt this was the break I had hoped for. It would definitely be a miracle to get it for my price. I was also blown away that within minutes of me stopping the search online and I had left it all to God, Carl had called me. I couldn't stop smiling. This was the sign of hope I had been waiting for. I felt it; I knew it and I simply believed it!

Two days later Carl called me again and said he had talked to his parents. They had a few vacant apartments and they would rather have someone in them than not. He offered to give me a one bedroom for the same price as I was paying in Edmonton for the two bedrooms. I was in tears!! They gave me a discount of $600 a month. He said he would not raise my rent unless I could afford more. I am not using his real name because he wouldn't want me to but he and his family deserve a mention of deep appreciation from me.

Miracles can happen, big or small when I simply keep my Faith and follow God's lead instead of worrying and stressing. As soon as I stopped worrying and getting frustrated online and left it all to God, He showed up for me again. Carl kept his promise and has not raised my rent in five years now. I am beyond grateful! I pray I can do something just as wonderful for him and his family in the future.

It makes me so happy when this happens and it's happened for me so many times when I am in the right head and heart space. When I'm surrounded in darkness is when I learn the hard lessons of not staying in my faith. That day my faith was strong and it paid off.

Lessons can keep coming back to us sometimes until we get it, especially if we are stubborn. *grin* Once we figure out why the same challenges keep looping around to us again and again, is when we finally learn the lesson. Only then will we recognize and stop the negative thinking and behaviour. It works every time for me. The simple answer to all struggles is faith. Worrying and stressing brings nothing but more of the same. I know this deep in my heart. That day I felt I was bestowed a great blessing for leaving it completely in God's hands.

Within a couple of days Carl sent me pictures of the apartment and the place looked great! The rooms are actually a little roomier than my last place because it's not a two bedroom but has about the same square footage. The bedroom is very roomy with two big closets. GREAT!!

After I let my children know it was final and I had found a place, all while trying my best not to feel guilty, I lined up a moving company. I could tell my kids weren't thrilled but they all said they understood. I do know they always want the best for me.

I knew I was taking a big risk putting this move on my credit card. A risky move no doubt but I had to take it for hopefully a happier future. My faith had already worked in my favour by providing the miracle of getting me an apartment for an unheard of rate in Fort McMurray. That alone had only confirmed for me that I was making the right choice. Little did I know there were plenty more tough times to come, but in that moment in time I was thrilled!

That last winter in Edmonton just two months after I had hurt my back, I had also connected with a man named Wayne online. I had already decided I wanted to move before he showed up in my life. I had promised myself if and when I did move it would be for me and not for him and I did just that.

Chapter 11

FREE AS A BIRD

I made the big move September 28th, 2019 and it went well. Other things, maybe not so much but I was happy I moved.

Almost a year later on July 10th 2020 I was sitting by a pond on my favourite park bench here in Fort McMurray, just a couple of blocks from where I now live. There were no clouds to be seen and the sun was shining so bright. I sat in my happy place, still flat broke and going through some things but at that very moment I felt content and I was smiling. I was happy to be there and to enjoy a few moments of peace. I live for those kinds of days where I am deep in my faith. The no-worries-be-happy state of mind. Some things in my world might have felt it was falling down around me but I at least felt good in that moment as I sat there meditating. I was having a good day and I relished every moment. We were in the middle of covid 19 and everyone was struggling in some way at that time. I looked for opportunities to take myself out of the chaos and fears, and in that very moment I felt at peace.

Diane M. Waterman

I tipped my head back to look up at the clear blue sky and I saw two seagulls flying very high in the sky. I had to focus on them for a moment before I figured out it was seagulls. They looked so tiny and the sun was making their whiteness aluminate against the blue sky. I could tell they loved their journey that day. They would flap their wings for a moment and just coast for a long time in their path going around and around in big circles. They were happy and healthy and living in the moment 'knowing' they were okay. I thought about what it must be like to be a bird and to be able to always know that what was needed would come. No ego tormenting their daily tasks. I'm certain they never worry about where their next meal is coming from. They just know it will come. This is the meaning of Faith. "Knowing without seeing."

There are people that live like the birds because they have learned how to live in the moment with not a care in the world. They live in peace even in hard times. That has been my goal as well. It doesn't come naturally for most of us but to even get close to that state of mind for moments or if I am focused enough for an hour during a day, is lovely. I've done it often over the years. To stay in it continuously when chaos surrounds me is a work in progress. I continue to work at it.

I do feel I am way more evolved than I was even five years ago. Most of us are. With age comes wisdom, for most. The work and determination to do better has saved me from myself many times. It would be easy to give up and just go to bed and stay there. Most of our society was living with day to day stresses. It is hard not to with so many crazy things going on in our world, especially today. We've all been through a lot.

Ask any monk and I'm sure they would tell you it takes many years of practice to get out of their ego and into living in daily bliss and peace. They don't let anything negative affect them. They care about what's going on around them and in the world I am sure, they just don't let it get attached to them.

God knows I've had many moments of that kind of bliss because I have had years of happiness and I have had so many happy times in learning and trying new creative things as well. I have had many good times with my friends, my family and meeting new people over the years. I have a ton to be grateful for.

The more time I spend alone now the more I work on taking care of me and hopefully others too, at least through my writing. We should all use our gifts even more as we have more free time when we age. It can take us out of our loneliness and in a more fruitful place of still finding some kind of joy, satisfaction and a sense of accomplishment in our golden years. We are not meant to just waste away as seniors. It can be a time to flourish and enjoy life even more. After raising our families and working hard for so much of our lives it's our down time to do what we want for us and others if we choose. I do enjoy finding peace and joy in the little things more and more as I was in that very moment.

Diane M. Waterman

I find my most peace while in meditation and in nature, away from all distractions. When I do reach those moments of stillness it is the best feeling in the world! I practice letting go of negative debris daily in my meditations. I strive to live like the birds and coast through life without worry knowing everything I need and want will show up like the many times it has in the past and to trust that God knows what is best for me. Sometimes what we think is best for us, really is not. I've learned that much.

Life will throw us a curve ball to learn from and sometimes surprise us in wonderful ways if we just let it happen. Worrying blocks that flow. To be able to rise above the trials and tribulations and watch it pass by, like it always does, is a great tool for survival of any kind of test. We still need to feel what we need to while knowing it will pass and get easier. The older I get the more I believe it is all a test in being a human being. The best parts and worst parts all depend on our perceptions of how we look at life. If we are really evolved there are no worse parts. There are just experiences we learn from. I am not that evolved yet, far from it but I have learned enough in some of my experiences to try and at least teach a few things.

I have learned that even in grief I know that my loved ones are waiting for me and they don't want me suffering here. That has helped me cope tremendously with loss and has helped me push through those times while still feeling all I need to feel. Without a doubt I know I will again be with my family that has passed.

Today being the anniversary of the loss of my sister Mona my heart squeezed tight. I felt she was sitting next to me watching the beautiful sky and the two seagulls dancing in circles. I even wondered for a brief moment if the birds were her and my sister Donna teaching me to let go and be free of all worries. I have had many signs from them.

In those moments when I was focussed on the birds I felt I was being taught something new. My smile was genuine, no mask. I have known this truth about my thoughts controlling how I feel daily and how they affect my whole life for a long time now. Why can't I just stay in that place of trust constantly throughout my struggles and not worry or ever be in fear? I try, God knows I try. It is because I am a human being, part human, part being. The human part is where the ego lives and can cause stress. On days like that special day when I 'just am' and I succeed at just taking in the moment is when I feel I am more the 'spiritual being' part of me than the human part and it's when I feel more at peace and closer to God.

Look at what those special moments watching those birds taught me when I stopped, looked up, took a deep breath and focused my attention on my surroundings. I am grateful for this lesson that I would have never learned with my head downwards staring at my phone screen. Most times on my walks I never take my phone. It is my time of peace.

I am pretty sure there aren't any birds or any kind of animals that sit around all day and worry about the monthly bills or what if I can't take care of me? What I was watching in the sky that day was total freedom from the ego that torments us humans from living our best lives. It was a beautiful moment and a great lesson in faith to take in and now share with you.

God knows my heart and soul had been going through a lot at this time since I had met a man on a dating site who had stolen my heart eighteen months before. I needed these moments of release from my thoughts now more than ever.

I truly believe all the talk we hear about in these times of many of us moving from 3D to the more beautiful and peaceful 5D (a shift in consciousness from a lower, more material focused state to a higher more spiritually attuned state) timeline is simply moving from our head space to our heart space, like the animals. That is the great awakening we all long for.

The school of life is never ending.

Keep Going.

Chapter 12

THE MARRIED MAN

I am writing the truth about a 'situation' that challenged me in so many ways. I have now learned some knowledge to maybe help others who have been caught up in something similar that can be so exciting one moment and then turn into something heartbreaking and so unhealthy. My truth will hopefully help someone else to not feel ashamed or as alone as I did. I learned a hard lesson and I am sharing because I no longer feel any shame at all. I know it was not a situation I would have ever chosen for me. Sometimes we simply fall into a trap. Never in a million years would I ever choose to purposely hurt me or anyone else this way, not even my worst enemy.

I believe God knows our intentions and that is the most important fact for me. I know my intentions while falling into this trap were pure. After a few years of torture in my heart and soul I have finally found some peace. In finding that peace I also found the courage to now share the experience with my readers.

Diane M. Waterman

As the years flow by us we are faced with more and more experiences to learn from. We tend to share the good ones easily. We can find the courage to share the hard ones or keep secrets and live our lives living in shame and guilt. That's not me and I intend to do neither.

I am a true believer that things are meant to happen for a reason or purpose. What would we learn without these hard experiences and lessons? Nothing. How could we share and teach to help others? We couldn't. When we survive a hard challenge and can get to a place of being grateful for the experience, because many times we receive more good out of it than bad, if nothing else we have more knowledge to relate to one another. Our compassion and tolerance expands. When we use the word experience instead of mistake we can use it without placing any judgement. Some will still judge and that's okay too. That is not my business.

On January 25th 2019, I had just gone back on a dating site that I had been on many times over my single years. I never stayed on there long, getting frustrated with the same games far too many times. I was aware and I was cautious knowing there were many liars and so many fake accounts trying to take advantage of lonely women and men in one way or another. I know the men get it too. I had heard it all and seen it all on online dating over the past years since my ex-boyfriend Gary and I had officially broken up as a couple in 2007. We stayed friends and companions for years after but both agreed we should look for someone more compatible. I wanted to find someone I could trust to share my life with. He had broken that trust many times lying about his gambling addiction. Other than that major issue, he was a good man.

Normally over the years after I joined the dating site I would stay on for a couple of weeks but then take myself off for months at a time before I would get overwhelmingly lonely and go back on. Sometimes I would hear from a man that I would have good conversations with about life and I did enjoy that part of it. Most times they lived too far away. I had no intentions of having a long distance relationship. In the many years of being on and off there I had been asked out to meet local men many times but only agreed to meet six men in person in that first year. That's not a lot considering hundreds ask. I know friends who would meet six in a week. Not kidding! I didn't have time for that. Five of the men I met in that first year I had no connection with and I remained just friends with one. After that first year I was turned off from meeting anyone else for some time, and then in 2009 I met up with one more man from a dating site that I did like and have remained friends with but we were not meant to be anything more than friends. He is happily married now and I am happy for him. I had politely turned down any other men who said they wanted to meet me but stayed on and off the site while still keeping a glimmer of hope for some kind of a miracle. I am aware it is very rare, at least for me, to find a true connection. I do try to stay hopeful.

I did meet a man I had a strong spark with in 2013 while out one night listening to friends play at a club. I wrote about him in *You Have to Go Now*. That friendship lasted four years but was not met to be for many reasons. I found out he was messing around with his ex was one reason. I loved him dearly and was heartbroken for a while after it ended. He started calling me shortly after I moved back to Fort McMurray and he asked to come live with me. I felt by his calls he had realized what he had lost. I politely said "No, I don't have those feelings for you anymore." He said he understood. I havent' heard from him since. I do wish him good things.

I have become aware in recent years that I have more barriers up now than ever before. There is no doubt that trust is something I struggle with because I have been let down in every relationship from my past, but I do work on keeping my heart open. I do feel if a trustworthy man that I really liked came along I would still give him an honest chance. I believe no matter how old we get most of us still desire to love and to be loved. It is one of the main reasons we are here in my opinion, to experience love of every kind, family, friends, animals and that one true love we all long for. Some of us find it, many don't. Even after letting each relationship go I have stayed optimistic over the years, but definitely have my guard up while still keeping an open mind and heart. It would take a real pro to fool me again and believe me, they are out there.

It was on that day in January 2019, just two hours after I went back on the dating site, that a man reached out to me that changed my life for the next three and a half years, and probably forever. I had been having the thought to go back on that day after being off there for months again. I had been fighting it in my mind. It kept popping in my head that day to try one more time. In the end I felt nudged enough by the Universe to give it another try and so I did.

I had also been told by a respected psychic just two weeks earlier that there was someone new showing up for me within the next four weeks, a new love. This part I wrote the truth about in my novel, *The Married Man*. For anyone that read that novel, it was fiction sparked by this new man I was about to fall head over heels for.

The psychic had described this man to a tee and sure enough it was two weeks later that Wayne contacted me just two hours after going back on the dating site. Wayne was the name he used on the dating site. I knew instinctively he was the reason I was nudged to try again. I instantly felt when he sent me his first two photos that he was the reason I was meant to go back on there. In all the years I had been on this site I had never saw anyone's photo that affected me instantly the way his did. The spark was instant just as the psychic had said it would be! After we talked for a while I found out the only thing the psychic got wrong about Wayne was that he was a widower. Wayne told me he was single.

In the future when I would find out he was married, this made no sense to me at all how the psychic could get every other little detail correct about this man and that most important thing wrong. He got his age, his height, his hair, teeth, yes he even said he had all his teeth, the instant connection and everything else was correct. Telling me he was going to be a widower just didn't make sense to me.

Over the many years I had been contacted by thousands of men online and I have viewed that many profiles as well, rarely reaching out to anyone myself. I'm a bit old fashioned and have always felt the man should make that first move. I know things are very different now and as independent as I have been I still am not comfortable with approaching men. I am open and friendly but I have never asked a man out on a date.

I had met thousands of men through work, my days of singing and going to dances in clubs over the past 28 years of being single. Even just going to a grocery store and seeing attractive men who might give you that look can happen. Nobody has ever once made me feel that spark as much as I instantly felt with this man. And it was only his photos. Even my handful of lifetime relationship ex's, that were all nice looking men, couldn't compare to the physical connection I felt right away to this man. It was electric physically and what was even more exhilarating and a little scary was that I also felt an emotional connection very fast. I felt it even more so after we messaged because I felt he was witty and sweet. The connection was easy and strong. I whispered, "Wow! He finally found me!" Lust is nice but I instantly knew somehow this was going to be deeper for me. And we hadn't even met in person yet…so I thought.

I consider myself very cautious and an intuitive person. I can usually tell right away if an account is fake or if the person I'm talking to is married or in a relationship. I saw a red flag on his profile. He had no profile picture up. He had sent me the two photos privately within minutes. I asked the questions and he responded to my doubts. I know there are people who don't want to show themselves openly on dating sites because of work. His reasoning seemed genuine at the time so I gave him the benefit of the doubt not wanting to push him away. I know my lack of trust can sometimes mess things up so I kept an open mind. My guard was up but falling fast.

I loved the photo's he had sent. There was one of him in the winter while out hunting and one of him in a coral color, muscle shirt. The physical attraction between us was so strong I know now it distracted me from clearly seeing the truth. I was still cautious and watched for any signs that he might not be living alone. How soon he was getting back to my messages was a big one and he always got back to me within minutes.

Diane M. Waterman

I watched for if there was a difference at certain times of the day as to when I heard from him. I saw no signs of anything off. He was consistent in his texting back and forth every day.

I wanted this to be the real so bad. We hit it off right away, in every way! The most attractive qualities I love and that are aphrodisiacs for me are intelligence and funny, and he had both. I love quick wit and so does he. We played off each other's humour perfectly. The spark is next and there was no doubt for either of us that it was there big time! "When it feels too good to be true, it usually is." That old cliché is not only true but sad because it usually means someone is getting hurt.

Chapter 13

THE SHOE DROPS

Two months later after talking daily, Wayne called me up and admitted the truth he was married only after I found evidence online. By then we were already madly in love. I fell in love with him faster than ever before with anyone but I didn't tell him that until after he had already said it to me just weeks into talking. For anyone who has never experienced love at first sight this would be hard to believe but it was far more than the instant attraction for me. My feelings for him grew quickly. I tried really hard not to fall fast because even though we were in contact every day, over time I started to feel something was off. I asked all the right questions from the beginning and he gave the right answers but by the end of two months I became aware that his daily routine of contacting me would change a little on weekends sometimes. I saw a red flag I couldn't ignore. When I would ask him about it he always had an answer but still something was not sitting right with me. I did what I had to do to find out if my intuition was right. I wanted so badly just once for it to be wrong.

Wayne had a family member pass away weeks after we connected that he had told me about. It took about another month before I saw the obituary online. His real name AND his wife's name were in the obituary. The shoe dropped!! Not only was I totally dumbfounded that he had lied to me with such conviction but how sad it was that I had to go to this extreme to find out the truth.

When I saw his REAL first name, right away I remembered that I had met him eighteen years prior to this. It was why he looked familiar to me. In the beginning he had already told me his last name truthfully when we first exchanged numbers and he had told me his family member's first name that had passed. He was honest about most things. If I didn't know that much I wouldn't have known the truth for some time to come. I can't imagine how that would have turned out. Even at my age and after knowing many liars in my life it still amazes me how people can lie so easily to get what they want. Changing his first name had definitely thrown me off.

His first name was unusual for a man and it had come to my mind briefly before this probably because of seeing the resemblance from my memory of him from years before. I had thought about him a few times over the years since our first brief encounters in 2001. I had wondered what happened to him and here he was talking to me daily and winning over my heart for more than two months.

As soon as I saw his real name on the obituary it sparked a memory for me and I remembered clearly that Wayne had tried to get involved with me when I worked at a jewelry store in Fort McMurray back in 2001. He had come to the store three times. The first time he was just walking by and he made a funny comment about seeing me yawn and stopped to chat to me. Sparks were flying!! The second time he dropped by the store just days later and he asked for my number. He went on to tell me he was married. The attraction was instant and strong back then as well but at least he had told me the truth right away. I never let it go anywhere as much as I was attracted to him. I point blank said, "No, I'm not interested."

"Okay sorry." He replied and walked off.

Two months later before Christmas to my surprise he returned to the store and stood in front of me outside the showcase I was working on. We both just stood there staring into each other's eyes for a minute or two. He turned around and left without saying a word. I never saw him again for eighteen years, until now. Wow! This was a lot to take in and the worst was yet to come!

I believe I am fairly intelligent and it was certainly not my first experience in life of being conned by a man but never in this way. I had much to learn. I wish my heart had been smart enough to close on him right away but I was in too deep now and that was not our journey.

People come into our lives often for contrast to give us choices in what we prefer. It's up to us who we choose to stay and who we let go. The morals we set for ourselves can be hard lined and can take the longest to mend and forgive if we break them. Now I had to make a choice, a hard one. It was certainly not my first time knowing I would have to let a man I loved go because he didn't match up to my standards when it came to honesty and integrity. The question was how long would it take this time?

I already knew this was going to be a challenge like none before. I was not okay with this at all. Love is not something we expect to happen whenever we meet someone, it just happens. What now?! Here it was eighteen long years later and this time he didn't tell me the truth up front to stop me from feeling this deep love I now felt for him.

As we continued the conversation on the phone we talked about my memories of meeting him before and he said he now remembered it too. I went on to tell him I had read the obituary online. I first said some kind words about his family member and how sad it was. I was very sincere and my heart did break for him and his family. I know how it feels to lose close family members. He thanked me and then I told him I saw his real name and his wife's name next to it. His response was, "You got me." I was dumbfounded by his response because he genuinely seemed defeated while still caring and kind towards me. He was not mad at me at all because I hadn't trusted him. I guess I was expecting him to somehow turn it on me. That is the gas lighting I had been used to from past relationships. I thought he would hang up on me and I would never hear from him again. He did the total opposite.

It didn't suit the character of the man I had fallen for to do something so deceitful. I had been with big liars before no doubt but never with a married man. I had offers from married men over the years of wanting affairs. I always turned them down. I knew I was worthy of much more.

I whispered, "Oh dear, oh dear." My heart was broken and my brain was on overdrive! I knew what I had to do now but it would not be easy. "So this is it then, we can't go on with this." I said. The tears started to flow. I was completely heartbroken!

"I'm sorry. I'm an assh**e." He said.

"Yup." I replied.

Wayne lived in Fort McMurray and I lived in Edmonton at the time so I was at least happy I found out before my move. The connection and pull to him was stronger than anything I had ever experienced in my 62 years. It was magnetic! To some people it may be seen as lust but for me it was much more than just our physical spark. He told me he felt the same. It was his tender and loving side that I had connected with the most. He was easy going and laughed at my sarcastic humour. I was totally me when talking to him. It was a strong, emotional bond and now I felt completely torn into! I wait forever to meet someone I feel connected to this way and now I can't have him?! It was cruel!

Wayne using a different first name had certainly thrown me off the most and his looks had changed somewhat after eighteen years. He also never told me his last name when I had first met him. I had only talked to him in person maybe fifteen minutes total in 2001. He now had gray hair and had filled out more physically.

I knew he was being honest about other things because he had told me many things he didn't need to, just not the most important thing he should have told me right away like he had done almost two decades before.

Then the bigger blow came after he had admitted he was not only married but for the second time since I last saw him. To whom he was now married to absolutely floored me! When he told me she used to sing in a band in town too, my mouth dropped open! To find out that the woman he was now married to is someone I used to sing in a band with back in the mid-nineties blew my mind completely!

After we affirmed we were talking about the same woman I was in even more disbelief! "Why her of all people?!" I cried. He kept saying he was sorry and asked me why I had that reaction to her. I clearly knew her. I calmed down enough to fill him in.

Kitty (not her real name) absolutely hated me and did everything she could to get me to quit the band because she was insecure, of what I don't know, but she made it clear she was by her actions back then. I filled Wayne in on how I knew her and how it became so tense in the band back then from all her stunts to undermine me that she got her wish and I finally quit. I was heartbroken at the time; tortured for months on what to do. We played at different venues for almost three years. The more people complimented me on my singing the more she seemed to hate me. I started to even ignore or brush of people's kind words towards me when she was around because I could feel the tension and see the glares coming from her eyes. Looking back now I should never have pulled back my shine for her. If it was at this time in my life I would have never done that. She got many compliments as well but it wasn't enough. She clearly hated me and no one saw it but me. Being a people watcher all my life I don't miss much when it comes to people's facial expressions and actions.

I felt I had no choice in the end but to leave the band. Of course looking back now I should never have tried to conceal my talent in order to make her happy and I should never have quit. Lesson learned. Wayne listened to me as I went on to tell him some of the things she had done not only to me but to my family. His response was, "Yes, she is very insecure."

Singing was something I had so much passion for and this was the first band I was ever in. I loved it so much but I could not stand being a part of something that was causing tension with the whole band. I felt no real support back then. Our friends and my family I had talked to about what she had been doing over that time period didn't want to hear it. They thought she was sweet as pie and couldn't see through the act. I have shared the stage with many female singers over the years that I love and they love me. There was never any jealousy, just support and so much fun! It was very hard for me to fathom anyone being any other way until I met Kitty.

During the years as a group we often went to hear other bands and we would hear fantastic female singers. I would always compliment them. Not once did Kitty say a nice word about any of them. It took me some time but I had finally figured her out and had her number. When I witness anyone who is so insecure that they would walk over anyone to be worshipped it really makes me feel sad for them.

I will give one example of a stunt she pulled multiple times that really boggled my mind. I'm not going to talk about everything she did. I just want to be clear on what I was dealing with back then and why I reacted like I did.

The last months the band was together Kitty would find out which new songs I was learning to sing with the band. Kitty would surprisingly show up at rehearsals with the same song on tape for the band to learn. The first time I was shocked that we had chosen the same song to do. Of course I didn't make any fuss and she did the song. Was this a coincidence? I asked my sister Donna if she had innocently mentioned the song I was learning to Kitty. She said she might have. They did work together and were best friends. I know at first I wasn't paying attention to mentioning new songs I was learning around her either because I never expected anyone to do such a thing as to undermine me that way.

Over the next few months I could clearly see it was no coincidence after it happened three times in a row. Tension in the band was building as she continued the behaviours. We were speaking less and less. This was all new to me and I didn't know how to handle it. Friends and family didn't believe what she was doing. She had them all wrapped around her finger. The only person I could talk to about it that would listen back then was my ex. I rarely saw him have sympathy for anyone but he did comfort me on this because he saw the tears I shed over it. I was really tortured on not wanting to quit the band over it because I really loved singing.

Before that last rehearsal we had together as a group I had purposely told Kitty the week before when we were all at a dance at the Legion what new song I was learning that week. I wanted to test her and make sure my intuition was correct about her and it was not a coincidence she had been showing up at rehearsals with the new songs I was learning. It was still hard for me to fathom anyone would do such a thing on purpose but I had to be certain.

Sure enough she showed up rehearsal night with song in hand on a tape that I had told her to her face the week before that I was learning for the next practice. She slyly gave it to the band leader before I even had a chance to mention it to them. That was the fourth time in a row. There was no doubt in my mind she was doing it on purpose. It was also the last straw for me. I was ready to face her. To stand there and listen to her practice the song with the band that night was almost out of body. I was fuming inside! Not because I felt I owned the song but because I couldn't understand the underhandedness of it all. Of course over time it became clear to me. She wanted me out of the band because she wanted all the attention on her alone.

I calmly and quietly asked to speak to her outside when rehearsal was over. There was so much tension in the band by then you could cut it with a knife. It had been building for months. I was being torn apart on what to do. Unexpectedly our lead guitar player followed behind us and was there as a witness. I was happy afterwards that he did because when you are talking to someone you know in your heart is not trustworthy we should always have a witness. I also know the only important witness is God.

I spoke calmly and asked why she had been repeatedly doing

the underhanded things she'd been doing. When I asked about the songs she kept saying "It's just a song." I replied, "It's four times in a row you did this?" I got no real answers from her, just the run around, so I left. She was not someone I wanted in my life anymore. My mind was finally made up. As sad as it was to give up the band it was also a relief to be away from ever having to deal with her again, so I had thought...

A close friend of mine since high school who was also friends with Kitty at the time this all went down, told me that shortly after I had quit the band they were all hanging out at a local bar. My friend said she approached Kitty and asked where I was? Kitty replied, "Diane is a f**king bit**!" My friend turned around and walked away from her. My friend didn't know yet that I had quit the band. I had not told anyone but my immediate family up until then.

Kitty clearly wasn't used to being called out for her conniving ways and by her cursing on me and calling me names to others after I had confronted her about her actions showed she definitely didn't like that I had done it. She had probably hoped I would just walk off into the sunset and not say a word to her or anyone else about what she had been doing. She had already convinced everyone else she was an innocent kitten. I saw through her acting and I believe now that was another reason she didn't want me around. I saw a lot.

You can bet she especially didn't like that our guitar player had tagged along at that last rehearsal when he overheard our conversation. The good part was she couldn't deny it in front of him. I felt really good that I stood up to her for her bad behaviour towards me, even if it meant giving up my passion. She didn't get what she wanted in the end because the band only played one gig after that and the band broke up.

Sometimes calling people out on their actions and doing it calmly and with class is worth more than any amount of gold and I at least felt good about that. She of course continued calling me the bit** after and spinning her own story about me as I expected she would have. I didn't care. I was told many times over the years by co-workers and by friends that I was too nice when anyone was disrespectful towards me. I was still learning to no longer be a door mat for people and to always respond in a straight forward and respectful way. That works for me. Not so much for the person I have to face. I still tolerate a lot before I step up but I always feel good afterword's when I do. I don't belittle the person I'm speaking to and I stick to the facts.

I didn't want this to turn this into a 'bashing another woman just to be vengeful' tell all because it's not. There was a lot more going on at that time that I could write about but won't. Again, I feel I needed to give you an idea of what I was personally dealing with at the time and why I felt the way I did about the woman that I had just found out was married to the man I had believed was single and loved. Mind blown is an understatement!!

Nobody, including my sisters, had my back or saw through Kitty's act when I had warned them not to trust her back in the nineties until shortly after I quit the band. In a turn of events Kitty not only hurt me but she then betrayed both of my sisters. I won't say what she did but I will say a male family member was involved. Kitty being married for the second time back then didn't ever stop her from going after what she wanted and she didn't care who she hurt to get it. I saw it many times. Hurting my sisters was a bridge too far for me. Things sure changed between my family and friends with Kitty after that. I didn't blame them for trusting her the way they had. She was cunning and she was a master manipulator.

My one sister still had to work with her every day after the bomb was dropped. Both my sisters were completely heartbroken by Kitty's betrayal because they had loved her. People can only hide themselves for so long and the truth will always prevail in one way or another.

I was at my sister's home the day after she had found out Kitty had betrayed them. My sister was so angry when she was venting to her husband about the whole thing she slammed her hand on the table at one point and said "I believed that bi*** over my own sister!" I sat there and didn't say a word. I didn't need to.

I had a lot to be angry about back then and those old feeling about Kitty were all suddenly coming to the surface again after talking to Wayne. How would I now deal with this new information that the single man I fell head over heels in love with was not only married but to this woman?! It felt like I was kicked while I was still down, first in the heart that he was married and then kicked in the gut as to whom he was married to! There are no other words to describe how I felt other than devastated!

Kitty sure caused a lot of damage and pain for me and my family in those years we knew her. Both of my sisters had thought the world of her. Love can blind us no doubt. It was easier for me to see the truth back then because being an empath I had picked up on her negative energy towards me early on. She had conned them all, won them over and then stabbed them in the back without a care or worry to how it hurt my sisters and our friends who loved her. It took something that had nothing to do with me for them to finally see her true colors. I didn't need to say anything more to any of them about it. Kitty had solidified what I had warned them all about. I loved my sisters and friends dearly and they were all learning too so they were not to blame. Nothing they could do to me would ever change how much I loved them.

I have not met a woman yet that I have ever been jealous of, never will. I feel all women are beautiful. We are all unique and special in our own ways. I love, respect and admire women as a rule. I compliment and always try and uplift other woman. Very few times in my lifetime have I had a problem with another woman but when I have it sadly always seems to come down to deep insecurity. We all have some insecurity but for most of us it is not so much that we would hurt others intentionally.

Never in a million years would I have predicted the future to turn out as it did almost three decades later since I quit the band. I don't believe in revenge but I do believe in justice. Was this love between me and Wayne karmic justice for Kitty or was I simply being blinded by a charming con artist as my friends and family once were by Kitty? I had some hard lessons to learn in this one new event in my life and it was a crazy ride from beginning to the end! There were times I felt the whole event was being orchestrated by the Universe because I couldn't make this stuff up if I tried.

Could I have been vengeful as soon as I found out who Wayne was married to? Oh yes, believe me it was tempting to let her know right away. The problem is I don't have that kind of heart and I still had more to learn for some reason. I also felt it was Wayne that should step up and tell the truth. After all he was the one that was married.

I was in scary territory that I had never let myself get into over the almost three decades that I have been single. Getting involved with a married man was something I had managed to stay clear of. I had set high standards for me, even more so after my divorce. I didn't want to make another mistake in choosing a partner. And here I was now in love with a married man whose wife underneath her sweet façade, I only knew in the past as the devil.

This man captured my heart before I ever knew the truth that he was married. That was so unfair. This was already the love of my life in my mind, heart and soul. Now what?! It was the saddest and craziest scenario I had ever been in the middle of and one I couldn't dream up or wish on my worst enemy… and that would have been Kitty. The only woman in the world I had ever felt real distain for from my past.

Once Wayne had admitted he was married on the phone that day and to whom, I knew I could never be intimate with him. I said goodbye to him. My whole heart broke into pieces when I hung up the phone. I curled up on my bed and let myself sob like never before. It literally felt like someone was pulling my heart out of my chest. "Why couldn't it have been easy just once??" I cried.

Wayne sent me a text soon after that revealing call asking if we could still be friends with a tear emoji attached to it. I knew we were both feeling the pain. I couldn't fathom that he was hurting as bad as I was but I did feel he had a heart and he knew he had hurt me deeply and would miss me too. It was a lot for my brain and heart to process. I do believe he is kind and compassionate. What I would come to realize later on is he is also very much like his wife in being selfish.

Keep Going

I thought it over for a while and said yes to just being friends. I just could not imagine my life not ever talking to him again. He had brightened my world so much before the truth came out. I didn't want to part with him completely yet. I also knew and really believed I had a lot of will power and I had to accept we could be nothing more than friends. I could live with that. I feel more and more as I age that falling in love is more about how good we feel inside while we are in love, that natural high, than the person we fall for. That's why it's so hard to let go of that kind of joy once we have found it inside ourselves.

I had had some strong connections before with men that I stayed away from physically. Little did I know how much stronger this one would be. I also had no idea how much harder it would be to not touch once we met again because now the heart was in it but I hoped I could resist. We both had agreed we wanted to meet each other for a hug once I had finally moved. I couldn't wait to see him and hug him but I had made it clear to him there would be nothing more. He agreed. Foolish woman!

There is no crime in two people meeting and falling in love. It happens every day, yes, even married people. Many of us are not meant to have one partner our whole adult lives and the heart wants what the heart wants. Keeping secrets is what don't sit right with me. If you want to be together with someone else tell the truth. Getting Wayne to do that was not what I was expecting at all. I had really believed in my heart that he had loved me enough to make a change for us. Wayne did give me false hope for more. He'd have to live with that. Despite all that happened after I had made my choice to move back to Fort McMurray and even knowing now all I went through I don't regret the move because I knew I was here for more important reasons than Wayne. There have been so many benefits for me in general.

By the time I moved I had told two of my friends about him. Eventually I told five of my friends because if they asked about men in my life I just simply wouldn't lie. I couldn't tell a lie if it killed me and they all knew me well enough to know that. Not telling all the details sometimes we all do but to make up or tell an outright lie, nope, I couldn't and wouldn't do it. My friends all told me they would have slept with him already, especially knowing our history. I told them all I just couldn't do it. It wasn't right no matter how many ways I turned it around in my mind. Most of my friends knew his wife. We had all ran with the same circles of friends in the eighties and nineties.

In early October 2019, just two weeks after I had made the move back to Fort McMurray, Wayne text me and asked if he could come see me. I said "Yes!" No hesitation. I felt apprehension and excitement at the same time! My hands were shaking trying to put on a little make up. It had been almost two decades now since I last saw him back in 2001. We are the same age, both born in 1956. He still looked great in the photo's he had sent me. I hoped he would see past the extra wrinkles and my now slightly curvier figure. It was a nerve wrecking feeling knowing he was still with her and I was doing this but if this meeting went well I believed in my heart and soul that he would do the right thing and tell Kitty the truth.

At 63 years old by now and never being in this particular situation before of meeting up with a married man, I was still a little naïve when it came to how far people will go to get what they want. Wayne had kept telling me he loved me and made statements like, "It could work out." I really felt that if we just had a chance to see each other physically again and if he and I still felt as strongly about each other afterwards he would find his courage and tell her.

Giving up on my hope and faith in Wayne before I even saw him would be the death of a dream I had with this man. I simply wasn't ready. To still have any faith in him after the big lie was hard for me but I loved him enough to risk it. We don't get anything good in life without risks and we don't learn any solid life lessons without failure and pain. This I did know but little did I know the mixture of joy, bliss, agony and pain I had to face in the future for making this one big decision. Was it a wrong decision? I don't think there are any wrong decisions. Our paths are our own to learn from.

My friend Dinah told me one day when I was baffled by someone else's deceit, the reason I can never conceive that people can be conniving is because my mind has never worked that way. I believe she was right. I also know hurt people who haven't healed hurt people.

I loved Wayne so much I had chosen to hang in there. That was on me. The physical spark we had yet to connect on would be far stronger than it had been almost twenty years before when I first saw him because now there was love. No doubt I was in for a roller coaster ride like none before!

Chapter 14

PHYSICAL TOUCH

When I went to open the door to greet Wayne he was sitting in his truck. I waved with a smile as big as sunshine! All the nerves in my body were lit! He stepped out and looked at me with the biggest smile on his face as he started walking towards me. Other than the natural changes from aging he was as tall and handsome as I remembered. I noticed his walk right away with his feet turned out a little with every step he took towards me. My heart was beating so fast!

I will never forget how we hugged when he stepped inside the lobby door. We fit like a glove and it felt like we had known each other forever. I cupped his face and said "look at us with our wrinkles now!" Both of us laughed. As we walked to my apartment we couldn't stop hugging each other. I never expected the physical touch would be as instant and comfortable as it was.

Once inside we sat on my couch. Wayne wrapped his arm around my shoulder and we held hands. Everything felt natural and easy. I felt safe and felt like all of my guards had suddenly dropped in an instant. How could this not be right?! We talked and laughed and couldn't stop staring at each other's eyes. It felt like a dream. I did let him kiss me. It all felt easy in the moment as I conveniently let the fact that he was married leave my mind.

Was I planning this to happen right away? No! Was I in my right mind? Probably not! I was definitely in my heart space. Sparks were flying and I felt more electricity in my whole body when our lips met than I had ever felt before with anyone! I kept my senses enough to know that was as far as I was willing to go. I hadn't lost my mind completely. The first real tinge of guilt would follow later. The whole situation was completely unnerving!

My love for him was stronger than my will power at this point and I have a lot of willpower. Without a doubt I was now caught in a trap that I saw no way out of. I was very hopeful Wayne felt as strongly about us as I did. He promised he wouldn't lie to me again and I never felt he did once I found out the truth.

Wayne stayed for half an hour and then I had to let him go. It was one of the biggest challenges I have ever faced in my life not to sleep with him. I was determined not to cross that line I had drawn for myself! It was all bad enough to let him kiss him. I also knew we had to see each other first physically to make sure what we felt was real. The connection was what I expected and more. It was off the charts!

Surely he would tell her the truth now? After all, he had told me there was no longer any attraction for him in his marriage and that there had been no intimacy for a very long time. Did he go about it the wrong way looking for love on a dating site? He sure did. I still felt his good side outweighed his bad at this point because he at least admitted his flaw and took all accountability for it. Looking back I was also looking for excuses to not let him go yet.

The second time he came to see me we sat and talked again, the whole time holding hands. That kind of spark and feeling so comfortable in his arms was nothing I ever experienced with anyone. We matched in almost every way possible when it came to attraction and personalities. His great wit and humour matched mine as well as his tender side. I felt completely loved by him.

This time he looked me straight in the eyes and said "I love you." It was the first time he had said it in person. I was stuck for words. He snuggled his face into my neck and just stayed there. I was taken aback. I rubbed my fingers through his soft hair and tried to think of what to say.

"Well you f**king better because I have been through hell and back!" I replied. His head went back and he laughed hard and was slapping his leg.

"You're hilarious!" He said.

After we both stopped laughing, because I didn't expect that to come out of my mouth either, I looked at him and said, "I love you too." He kissed me tenderly over and over.

Then of course the guilt set in a little more when he left and was now starting to eat at me daily. Something had to give! This was the first time I started to feel that maybe his intentions might not be what I had hoped. I had hoped he would tell me right away he was leaving her after our first meeting. In my mind he had to know the physical was there as well as the love. What more did he need?! Intentions are everything and I was well aware God's eyes were watching. I really wanted to do the right thing but how darn long was this going to take?! I asked him at one point, "Do you think we would have to make love for you to know for sure how you feel?"

"No, I already know that would be great!" He replied.

I needed to ask these questions to try and find out where his head was at. I had no intentions of going to bed with him. I felt I would give it enough time for him to be sure without putting too much pressure on him. I could see he was struggling. I knew where my heart was already.

Over the next year Wayne came to see me many times. It was almost two years by then since he first contacted me online. I felt I had invested and given my whole heart and life for him by then. Each time I saw him in person was just as thrilling as the last but in the end the pain I suffered without him stepping up so we could be together was slowly killing my spirit. The guilt I was feeling was destroying me as the woman I had grown to love.

The last time he came to visit me things had gone too far and I knew then and there I had to dig deep and find the strength to stop seeing him before things got completely out of hand. Up until then I had stuck to my guns. I told myself that day that I had turned down many men in my life that I was attracted to and sometimes loved, all for the right reasons, to protect me and my morals. This one time I allowed myself to cross a line. I made up my mind I wasn't willing to give up another man I loved without loving him completely. I had standards I had set so high for myself that even Mother Theresa would have trouble holding them up. This one time I was allowing my walls of protection to come down while knowing my morals and standards I had set for me were taking a hit.

Somewhere down the road I would have to forgive myself because I know me and I know me well enough that this would never sit right with me. No matter how many times I told myself it was okay because there was love there, deep down I knew it wasn't. I felt I had followed the standards I had set for myself throughout my life and had worked hard to turn around and heal any mistakes I believed I had made. I had thrown caution to the wind that one day and gave into something that in my mind was bad. It was also wonderful because it is a memory I will have forever of something magical with someone I deeply loved. Yet, the part of me that knows me so well knew this was not the healthy love I so longed for. Love should not come with pain and guilt attached.

It was always me that pulled away and tried distancing myself many times, never him. It amazed me sometimes that he kept coming back to me and the patience he had with me. I'm sure most men wouldn't have waited that long to try and take a woman to bed. It seemed he would wait forever for me to let him touch me that way. Now I had to dig deep for the strength to pull away for good because the guilt that had set in was worse than I had imagined. I simply don't have it in me to try and be something I know at my core I am not. It goes against everything I believe in.

By then the suffering and pining for him was more than I could bear most days. If I didn't get control I knew it would completely destroy me. I was in a lot of darkness and suffering and it was affecting every part of my life. My self-esteem had been so damaged by this because I was not someone who could settle to be number two with anyone. Deep down I know my worth and I knew I deserved better. With him wanting to continue without making any change for us after me giving him my all, finished it for me. Somehow, someway, I had to save me!

July of 2022 Wayne called me to let me know his brother's

wife and his brother found out about us. I asked him if he regretted what happened between us because by now I had found out many people knew. "HELL NO!" He said with all confidence. He didn't seem too worried about it.

I don't regret loving him either but I knew if I let it continue any longer that little seven year old girl inside of me and that courageous woman that I had done so much work for and had grown to love would soon disappear completely into dust. I couldn't ever let that happen.

I threatened twice when I was in complete despair and at my lowest that if he didn't tell her I would. I hated doing that but I needed him to step up. He would plead with me not to do it and I would give in not wanting to hurt him, or even her. Neither one of us wanted to hurt anyone, yet I was being torn to shreds. As much as it might hurt I know we all deserve truth. I was at a point that I could finally accept he just wasn't going to step up.

I would eventually get to a point of taking my power back and to heal number one, hence this book helps. I am putting the work in to ensure this never happens to me again and part of my purpose for putting this out there is to make women more aware and cautious so it doesn't happen to them. I know there are others going through similar situations that will connect and hopefully find strength in whatever they need from my story. I always pray my truth helps someone else heal. I have found that sometimes there just is no figuring it out, it just is what it is; painful life lessons. I wouldn't wish this situation on anyone. It was a nightmare for me and I am sure for him as well on those days we were both hurting.

Courage does not come easy for many. Something that has become a turn off for me in some of my past relationships and what ended them for me is a man without courage to step up and do the right thing. It takes a lot of courage to be honest. I had been through and survived so many things in my life because of the one thing I know I have and that is courage. I could no longer tolerate this lack of courage in him.

Although me loving and continuing to see him was wrong in my mind and societies mind, only because he was married, loving him the way I did and feeling loved by him was one of the best experiences of my life. I also know it was the most painful to get over. "What don't kill us makes us stronger," is no joke.

I give myself a little bit of grace because I fell in love with a single man, so I was told and had cautiously believed. But to let it go on after the fact was wrong. I knew I needed to also figure out what was still flawed in me to let this affair of my heart and soul continue. I do know if I had known the truth from the beginning, like the first time we had met, I would not have given him a chance to get close to me. That is who I really am and that's why my heart and soul were so tortured.

Keep Going

I had good intentions when we connected. He did not.

I was starting to see the light and how I was vulnerable, lonely and yes manipulated. That was so hard to take in because I felt I was smarter than that and I wanted to believe he was better than that. The truth is I am human and it happens to many people. With this realization I now had to be the strong survivor that I know I am. It would become even more painful to keep my distance from him and it would take deep healing, forgiveness and yes so much strength to do the right thing.

Nobody wants to be weak and with him I became weak. I also believe love is love and nobody should have to fight it because of judgements from others. However, the best judge is how we feel inside and there were many days I didn't feel good at all. How we feel inside is where the answer always lies. My history shows that I was always against marital affairs and with good reason. I am now more against it than ever.

Letting go of Wayne would have been like letting go of my sister Donna who was also my soul mate. They are very much alike in so many good ways. There is no question I will always love his good side, his humour and his soft side. Their tender hearts are the same. I told him often he reminded me of her. Maybe it was harder giving him up because I already had suffered losing her and I didn't want to go through that kind of grief ever again. Therein lays the truth. Many times I get more clarity as I write. Tears are flowing…

I knew deep down I would never be okay with being deceitful. That is who I am. It is what I couldn't live with and that in the end became the end for me.

Every time I said good-bye to Wayne it was painful and I knew this last time was not going to be any easier. My heart felt tight and I felt like I would have a break down if I gave into my true feelings but I fought it every day. I said goodbye to him at least 45 times over a three and a half year period. I know it's hard to believe but if you asked him he would agree it was true. Every second week I would pull away from him and tell him goodbye. Within the next day or two he would text me and say hi or ask how I was and we were back to talking again. Then two weeks later we would go through the same cycle and I would say goodbye again. It was the craziest thing I have even been involved in. It was torture for both of us. He had me hooked and I obviously had him hooked.

I read in a magazine article one time that you can tell when a couple is truly in love because they are constantly looking in each other's eyes while talking. We never stopped looking into each other's eyes every minute we spent together. We would drink each other in. It was beautiful! I keep the good memories near and dear to me but have to also remember at the same time of how dangerous the whole thing was for me.

At one point before things got out of hand I had cried in his arms and asked him if there was anything I could do to make a difference for him to tell her the truth? He said "no, you've done more than enough." I agree. I had given up a lot to spend even five minutes with him. I had given up my most precious gift, my self-worth, briefly. Now I had to take it back. I knew my heart and soul had been damaged. I also knew I would work hard to make me whole and healed again.

My last book I wrote called *The Married Man* was released in December 2020. It was something good that came from my love for this man. He was my inspiration to write it. I loved him that much. I figured if I can't have him in real life I can still have my fantasy of him in a book. Writing it during covid was also a blessing that kept me busy and sane.

The Married Man was a gift to me and for him to at least remember no matter how messed up it was, there was love there. It is a fiction with ten percent truth. Like all of my books I didn't plan it. The title came to my mind and I ran with it. The ending took me by surprise because I didn't know where it was going until the very end in writing it. I was happy with it. I often feel now that novel might be the reason I did meet Wayne again. I am grateful I at least got that much out of the affair.

Wayne knew I was writing *The Married Man*. He knew the title and he was absolutely fine about it. I even ran his character's name by him that I had chosen and he approved. I asked him if he could have chosen a career other than the one he has what would it be? He said a helicopter pilot so I added that to the story. I know he did read some of it. Not sure if he read it all yet. He complimented me on what he did read at the time. He had told me several times he loved that I was intelligent and funny. He said, "You're a great writer Puss!"

How Wayne truly felt about us? I only know what I experienced and felt, not just his words. I do know his fears override a lot. I know I felt his love for me was genuine every time I was with him even when he didn't speak it. I also know he will say whatever suits the moment to cover his actions to his wife and family.

I was surprised to hear that a friend of mine had privately messaged and told Kitty the truth about Wayne and me in March of 2020. My friend saw that Kitty had read the private message on IG and that she had changed her social media account to private right away without responding to my friend.

As much as I don't have warm fuzzy feelings for Kitty I have never hated her and she did have a right to know. I would certainly want to know. I didn't know about the friend writing to her until after it was already sent. I saw the message with my own eyes after the fact. I wasn't mad at my friend for writing to Kitty. I understood she thought she was helping me at the time.

I told Wayne right away after I found out the message had

been sent. He said that Kitty didn't say a word to him and she was acting normal. He didn't believe there was a message sent to her because she showed no signs of knowing. There were other times he had told me about before this that they had big blow ups because of her insecurities yet she had brushed the information about me under the rug and ignored it. I found that very interesting and I wondered why? I believe now she never brought it up to him because she knows there are things that I know about her she wouldn't want to have to discuss with him. Her acting like nothing happened after receiving that message also showed how good of an actress she still is.

I have to admit I felt some kind of justice had prevailed knowing I was no longer a secret nor would I ever be again to anyone in the future. I told Wayne one of the last times we spoke that it gave me some kind of satisfaction that people know now. He said he understood where I was coming from. Kitty knows, her family knows, his family knows and now the world knows. After what they both put me and my family through both justice and forgiveness was important for me to finally be at peace. I at least changed their names. If this was a vengeful trip for me, I would not be protecting them at all. Taking responsibility and finding forgiveness for number one as well is the most important action for me.

Wayne and Kitty's family will have their own version of the truth to protect them (if any of them ever know of this being out there) and like most affairs of the heart I know I will be the one their family will most likely blame. The married man is rarely to blame to their family and friends. The single woman is always blamed even when she was lied to. That doesn't bother me because I know the truth, Wayne knows the truth and God knows the whole truth.

I will never be ashamed of falling in love but I do wish the one I fell for was honest in everything he did and said. At least then I would have had a choice to fall in love or not but as Garth Brooks sings in his song, "I could have missed the pain, but I'd have had to miss the dance." The dance at times was certainly painful but also lovely, tender, kind, fun, passionate, sensual and satisfying in the end! Was it worth all the pain too? It may not seem so in the next chapters but I would say now that I survived it all, "Yes it was!" The good memories I now have with Wayne are mine and mine alone to keep forever.

The contradictions, confusion and after effects of it all were worse than I could have imagined for some time to come in the healing process. I feel now it was something I was meant to experience in life to challenge my strength. God only knows I hadn't had enough difficult challenges already. *sarcasm*

Wayne has many wonderful qualities but his one big flaw hurt me tremendously. I could have been vengeful and tore his life apart at the time but what good would that do?! I wanted it to be his free will and choice to make a sacrifice for me and he didn't. If the circumstances were different and he did some healing work on him I feel we could have had an amazing life together. But that is the fantasy I dreamed of, not the reality I now live in. His wife brushes everything under the rug to keep him. Living the lie of a happy marriage is their act to perform. Many will believe it. The intuitive will see through it.

The end of November 2021 was the last time I saw Wayne physically when he surprised me and showed up at my lobby door to give me an early Christmas gift. He was in a hurry and did not come into my apartment. I have not seen him since then. It was almost like our souls already knew we wouldn't see each other again as we clung to each other passionately that day. There were lots of hugs and kisses and not wanting to let go. I also felt defeated every time he left me to go to her. I had enough!

I felt it in every part of my being the next day that it was time to stop the roller coaster and get off. My determination had set in even more and this time I knew somewhere deep inside my decision was final! What I needed to do the most was to find the discipline to change the habits and daily routines of contact with him. That would still take some time but at least I was making the right steps towards distancing myself and healing. Some days I couldn't see how I would ever survive it all but I would tell myself to Keep Going and to take one day at a time.

We would still send text and delete each other of our phones only to put each other back on again a day later, I don't know how many times, before that stopped too. He did wish me a Merry Christmas and in 2022 and 2023 we exchanged a few emails. We agreed to always stay friends and if something important happened we could reach out because we still cared. It made it easier for both of us than having to think we would never speak again. That bargain would have been just too final and too painful. The days, weeks and months that passed by with pulling away more and more from the man I felt at the time was the love of my life was beyond a challenge. It would change me forever in building my strength. Wayne stayed strong too in the end for me. If I did have a weak moment in between and cry to him in some of my worse moments he did his best to help me stay strong. Me loving me is the most important to me and I had to fight to get that feeling back again.

Now that I have learned more about human behaviour over the years my feelings for Kitty has changed as I have grown as well. I know it was actually her she hated back when we sang together. I had the confidence she lacked back then. I feel sympathy for her in writing that because she was talented and beautiful in her own way but she couldn't see it. Confidence is beauty! It has nothing to do with looks or talent. Now I had to heal the damage that was now done to mine.

I will take you back in the next chapters to some of the hardest struggles I learned from in this battle of the heart. It is important for me to talk about how hard it really got to hopefully save anyone else who may have taken this path, blindly or not. You may say in the end it's a journey you would never want to take and I would reply, "It was my journey alone to take." How could I teach such a lesson or help others without it?

I know I could have kept this love affair going for years to come with Wayne but my strong sense of self-worth that I never lost completely, wouldn't let me. My true self, my soul knows I deserve much more in life. I am happy to say by 2024 I am happy with me again and have definitely healed and grown from the experience. Every connection whether uplifting or challenging has its purpose that eventually will reveal itself. I know telling my truth will help me tremendously in finally letting it all go and moving forward in my life. I feel I can leave that pain behind me now.

I would hope and pray Wayne and Kitty have also learned a lesson, at the very least to never again mess around with and break a writer's heart with their bad intentions. They should know if they do it'll end up in a song, a poem or a book. After all, healing heartbreak through writing is an artist privilege and greatest gift. It is one that I am taking full advantage of for healing for me and others who may need help.

My lesson is to always be number one in my life and to never settle for less. I am worthy. Keep Going!

Chapter 15

THE BLUE ORB

It is important for me to write about how bad it got for me before I finally found my power and took myself out of the unhealthy love affair with Wayne.

Looking back to January 25th 2020…

It had only been four months since I had moved back to Fort McMurray and one year since I had first been contacted by Wayne. It was the first time I had given Wayne an ultimatum and said I was done after one year. Little did I know back then it was just the beginning of many goodbyes. I had also started writing *The Married Man*. I needed to express what I was feeling and what better way for me than writing a book?! It was at that same time I suddenly started seeing a blue orb around me.

The orb is a beautiful cobalt blue color. It's not a solid color. It is see through like a veil. I didn't pay much attention to it at first. I had no clue what it was. I first noticed it a few times a day. I would see this flash of blue to the left of my face. I had never seen anything like this before so I started trying to make logic of it of course. It's the first thing our human mind will do. I thought maybe it was a reflection off my TV or that my glasses were suddenly giving off some kind of weird glare. I ignored it for the most part. It wasn't until later that I realized that it had shown up the day I started writing *The Married Man*.

After that first year I thought I had finally pushed Wayne away for good. I never dreamed it would take more than another two and a half years of struggle.

Little did I know that this blue, glowing circle I was seeing was an actual orb. I had no idea because I had only seen white ones on videos or in photo's. I had also heard stories of people I knew seeing them. The thought had suddenly come to me after a few weeks of seeing it that maybe it might be an orb but still I couldn't understand at the time why I was suddenly seeing it and why it was near me many times a day?

I started to notice it more often the days I was really feeling the most sadness. I was totally heartbroken the day I started writing *The Married Man* because I had just said goodbye to Wayne on the phone and was in a space of believing I would never see him again. My broken heart was where the whole idea of the book came from and in wanting to remember how much I had loved him.

Some days I would see the orb up to ten times a day. After a few weeks I started seeing it not only by the side of my face but directly in front of me as I sat in my chair. Sometimes I would just look up from my laptop and see it just for a second. In time I saw it in the bathroom in front of me and sometimes in the kitchen. I was baffled but I knew by now it was not a refection off something. I started to feel it was a spirit guide. I also started to feel like it loved me and was helping me somehow. God only knows I needed the help some days. Between my finances and loving a man I couldn't be with, there were days the positive self-talk just wasn't cutting it. It took great will and fight to even get out of bed some days but I did, every day. On my better days I was still seeing it three or four times a day. It seemed to be about five to seven inches in diameter.

Around September 2020 I was watching a lady online who is quite popular and who is spiritually inclined. She was answering questions for her followers in a live feed. I felt she was genuine and the real deal from listening to her live videos a few times before.

I typed this question in the comment box. "I keep seeing a blue orb around me. Could you tell me if it is a spirit guide?" There were hundreds who were asking her questions so I knew it was the luck of the draw to get a response from the lady but to my amazement, she responded to my question.

She said, "Yes Diane. The blue orb is a spirit guide." Wow!

Keep Going

My instinct was correct. I was mind blown and happy that I at least now had an answer! I felt quite relieved that it wasn't something medical. I was also curious as to the name of my spirit guide. As many times as I asked during my meditations I had never received a clear answer because my mind can't be still enough to hear it. Our intuition will give us answers if we listen.

A few weeks later my son Jeffrey was doing a pod cast. He was interviewing one of my favourite spiritual mediums Ginette Biro. I trust her completely having experienced an amazing read from her before and most of my family has had reads from her. At one point during the podcast they started taking questions. I wanted to get another confirmation on my spirit guide who was around me every day now. So I typed in my question again asking if the blue orb I see around me is my spirit guide. To get another validation from someone I respect and trust would be amazing! I really wanted to know the name of my guide too but I didn't ask her that part. Ginette being the amazing intuitive she is picked up on that.

Again, I was blessed enough to be chosen to have my question answered. Ginette replied, "Yes Diane, the blue orb is your spirit guide. It is not your life time spirit guide but is your inspirational spirit guide." She then went on to say, "And give me a second so I can get the name of your guide… Constance is the name."

My inspirational spirit guide?! This now made total sense to me, considering it showed up on the day I started writing *The Married Man*. Wow! I have always felt my writing was being guided. Knowing this now would help me in trusting my intuition even more. I felt this was very special for my guide to actually let me see itself as an orb. I also felt it was looking out for me and protecting me somehow because I saw it more frequently on the days when I was very sad.

I responded to Ginette in the comment box. "Thank you so much and I love that name!" I was so thrilled and the best was yet to come!

The Universe nudged me the next day to Google the name Constance. My mouth dropped open as I stared down at my phone and saw the short version of the name. Even though it is more of a feminine name, the shorter version is the true name of the man who inspired me to write *The Married Man*. My body suddenly broke out in goose bumps!! Wow, wow, wow! This sudden revelation of how everything I was going through with this man was also spiritually connected touched me so deeply I wept! It made our connection and my book that much more special to me. It was clear to me now that all that had happened was no coincidence. For it to all come around and end up becoming another inspired book for me to write I came to truly believe it had been all orchestrated by the Universe. Mind blown!

Wayne would probably not take any of this seriously, yet,

because he is not a big believer in the afterlife and in spirit. We had had a few discussions about the spirit world. He isn't completely cut off from it but we just have had different experiences. I am open to it because I am a believer. I was so grateful to get answers for something so unique and amazing!

It is because of my life time of experiences with the spiritual world, premonitions and so on, that I do believe whole heartedly that this was very real and far beyond what many of us know or understand yet, but we will.

Being open minded and connecting with many sources of positive energy my mind and heart has opened up to a much broader spectrum of truths. My faith in the afterlife and the Universe has deepened even more over the years because of it. I've grown leaps and bounds because of my willingness to learn more from spiritual leaders who are wiser, more experienced and in tune with the Universe than I am.

This was just another revelation to me that my relationship with Wayne was something neither of us had experienced before and why it took so many attempts to pull away. We were truly like magnets. We were like one. I had thought I met my twin flame once before but it felt nothing like this and was not nearly as hard to pull away from.

It was a few days after Ginette answered my question and gave me my guide's name that I decided to send her a private message. I knew she had read *The Married Man* and I wanted her to know how amazing this revelation had been and what it meant for me to know this. I felt good and was happy that what I was seeing and feeling was real and had been verified by her and by Spirit.

I know Ginette to always be non-judgemental and always kind. I trust her. I told her the shorter, true version of this story. I had also told her how shocked and happy I was to find out the name of my inspirational guide. I felt it was not a coincidence that my guide had the same 'longer version' name as the man that had inspired me to write the fiction.

Ginette wrote me back and said, "This is amazing!!" She also told me she had often talked to people's higher-self while they were still living and she thought that Constance could be Wayne's higher-self guiding me and watching over me. She went on to say the blue orb was around me now as my guide because Wayne had 'missed the boat,' so to speak. This new information made me happy in my heart. If his higher-self loved me as much as to guide me and protect me here in our 3d world, that alone was all telling and profound! It also said a lot about his true spirit.

Little did I know Constance would show up even more when I would least expect it. No matter if I never spoke to Wayne again I now knew this deep connection I felt with him would never be broken spiritually. It made total sense to me now of how I was guided to write the ending of *The Married Man* the way I did.

Chapter 16

THE BRIDGE

In May 2021, sixteen months after I first saw the orb, I was really pushing myself to go for a walk because I was feeling more anxious than usual. I decided to go take a walk across the bridge just minutes from my home. I love walking across there. There is a great view of the sky that I enjoy every time I go there.

Even though stress can cause me physical pain, walking helps alleviate the stress which in turn lessons the pain. It's a cycle I have learned to control most days. Mental thoughts are everything in controlling daily pain for me because stressful thoughts and feelings trigger the fibromyalgia. I have to distract myself away from the negative thoughts as soon as possible, especially when it's thoughts and worries about situations I have no control over.

I was definitely in a sad place on this day but had not been aware of how really down I was. I knew my heart was hurting more and more from missing Wayne because it had been a few months since I last saw him and our communication was becoming less. I was trying to distance myself. I didn't realize that I was in trouble mentally. The longer I went without seeing him and talking to him daily I knew the closer I was getting to ending it for good and that also scared me. I missed him terribly. My anxiety was building far worse than I had realized in those weeks and months. I didn't want to lose him but I was losing myself so it had to stop. It would still take me months to change all routines but I had been really trying.

As I was walking across the busy bridge side walk and as I looked at the flowing water down below I felt I was beginning to feel even more anxious and these thoughts suddenly came out of nowhere. "I wonder how it feels to jump off this bridge. I wonder how many people have done it. It must be so scary?" Suddenly I became very alert and aware that I was asking myself these crazy questions! It scared me having these kinds of thoughts even enter my mind! Even though I was feeling weepy and my heart hurt so bad I never saw myself as really depressed because I could still get out of bed and function okay. I know now that is a misconception I told myself. I can still be functional and not well. I did know my heart felt more tight and heavy than normal. As much as I let myself feel a lot of what I was going through at the time I also tried shrugging the hurt feelings off many times just to cope. Never mind on top of this I still had the heavy burden of daily financial troubles and worries. When would this heartache and stress ever end?! I was more sick and tired than I had realized and these thoughts I was now having suddenly scared me awake!!

As I quickly turned around and started walking back towards home I looked away from the water below and to the cars coming towards me in the lane to the right of me. All of the headlights were suddenly glowing blue around the edges. I whispered, "What in the world is going on??" I would blink my eyes and continue looking at the headlights as each one passed me by but nothing changed. There were about ten or twelve cars at a time that would pass and they all had the same blue glow around the headlights. At first I thought it might be those headlights with the neon blue lights around the edge that I saw once in a while but that didn't even make sense to me. This was every car and truck. I had walked that bridge so many times and never saw this before. It baffled me! I wondered just for a second if it had anything to do with the blue orb I had been seeing around me for more than a year by then. I had been clueless in that moment of how sad I really was and how dangerous a moment this really was for me. As I kept walking and looked back down again at the river I suddenly felt the need to get off the bridge quickly! I heard that soft voice firmly say, 'Keep Going!' Once I was off the bridge the cars coming towards me suddenly had normal color lights. I was totally baffled!

I walked swiftly back towards home not looking back. I dragged my behind up the stairs to my apartment. I sat in my comfortable chair and let go of what I realized I had been holding in for weeks and months by then since disconnecting more from Wayne. He had also been what I felt like was my best friend that I had talked to daily and told everything too. I missed him deeply!

I covered my hands over my face and finally let myself sob openly to release the pain and strain I could feel that had built up around my heart. When I started to feel relief I knew I would be okay but I sure had a lot more work to do. Not talking about what I was feeling going through all of this had been building to the point of distress that I wasn't aware of until then.

That constant financial worry, the emotional heartbreak of losing loved ones that I trusted to talk to and now the pain over giving up another man that I loved deeply was bearing down on me more than I knew. I was scared, especially now in having those uneasy thoughts on the bridge that I was at a point that I would not be able to carry the load any further by myself. The pain was unbearable!!! I had to do something more, so, I opened my laptop to write. My saving grace! If this didn't help me I would have to get myself in to see a therapist for extra help to see me through this very difficult time in my life. I do know by now that writing my truth saves me and hopefully others!

If you are not a spiritual person you won't believe any of this about the blue orb and that is okay. I'm not trying to convince anyone of anything that they don't believe in or have not experienced themselves. This is my journey and I can only know and share about my own personal experience. I have had many different spiritual experiences. Constance was a brand new experience for me and one I valued and didn't take lightly. I truly believe that beautiful blue orb saved me that day. Everything happens for a reason or purpose...

After getting home safely and releasing my heart from the grips of total heartbreak I started to think about what I had just witnessed on the bridge. Thinking back to the information Ginette had given to me about the blue orb everything suddenly made sense and became clear to me. I came to have a much deeper appreciation for my inspirational guide after this instance. I felt with all certainly that Constance was not only my spirit guide but my protector as well.

Those cobalt blue lights I saw surrounding all the cars headlights had had me baffled in the moment. I now believe it was Constance. For some silly reason I felt the only place the orb could be was in my apartment. Why would I think that?! They can show up anywhere. Amazing what clarity comes with experience and when we open up our minds more.

I really believe that in those moments on the bridge when I was more broken than I had realized, Constance distracted and protected me from those dark thoughts. It was in that very moment when I looked down at the water and started having crazy thoughts that Constance surrounded me with its blue veil of protection. I believe that is why when I then looked back at the cars and trucks passing by me that all the headlights were suddenly the exact same shade of cobalt blue as the orb. In my mind there is no other logical explanation.

What a both scary and most beautiful experience to take in and to take serious! I believe it with all my heart and soul. That blue orb is Wayne's higher self, which is the biggest and purest part of him in spirit, who was now not only my inspirational guide but without a doubt in my mind, also my protector. That is profound!

I believe our spirit we live in as humans are only a small part of our higher self that awaits us on the other side. When we cross over we will connect back to our higher self again. The more I have learned about the spirit world the more I am convinced of this theory. I can actually say I have now experienced enough to believe it to be very real. We too often dismiss what's literally right in front of us because it's new or we don't understand it. Keeping an open mind and talking to others that have more experience than us in these areas can give us more understanding and clarity, if we are interested and open to it.

I have always been curious by nature and want to learn more in general about many things. Cutting ourselves off from learning more is a crime in my books. Many times we cut ourselves off from learning out of fear because of beliefs instilled in us as children.

Part of my healing now was to completely let go of all the dreams I had conjured up in my mind in the beginning of knowing Wayne. I had felt I had finally found the man of my dreams when I believed he was single. I never give up on my dreams. It is very hard for me but I saw no reason to hang on to this one any longer. I had to also completely let go of believing he would choose me in the end. I am not someone who's gives up easily but in this case I knew I deserve nothing but the best and he is not the man for me despite the strong connections.

I was missing and pining for the good side of Wayne that I felt so connected to that day. In this very moment as I write these words I have decided to take that love I poured into him, turn it around and give it to me! What a powerful and awakening moment when I just wrote those words! Give that same deep love to me! Yes!

I had let loving him take away from my own self-love that I had worked on building for so many years. Not anymore! More and more I am learning I am my one true love. I have to always take care of number one first. I deserve the best love and nothing less!

Keep Going

As time went on I learned to value myself more than ever before. Today, March 13th 2024, after doing many rewrites on this book, I have released so much pain. I feel I have come a long way in healing and finally have way more good days than bad. Right now I am number one in my life again and it feels stupendous! I believe everyone that is sent to us is sent for a reason to teach us something about us. The challenges these encounters can take can be some of the hardest in our lives but look at what we learn. We learn the value of what each lesson brings us and how much it strengthens our character and self-worth even more once we make it out the other side. I thank God I made it.

I still see glimpses of Constance when I am writing but not near as much now. I guess my beautiful spirit guide feels I am doing okay on my own. And as I just wrote that last sentence I saw a flicker of blue light to the left of my face. *big smiles* They hear our thoughts all the time.

My financial situation was still another story. One day at a time. Keep Going!

Chapter 17

MORE HUMILITY

Even though I thankfully got through the agony of letting go of the man I loved I still had work to do to survive the financial crisis I was in at the same time. I work hard to be a survivor and not a victim. I have witnessed people who seemingly have happy go lucky lives because they constantly sweep things under the rug. That will eventually come back to bite you where it hurts in one way or another. They wear a mask. I have certainly been there so I recognise it in others. Many end up turning to unhealthy behaviours to cope. Some become addicts or worse. Without facing reality and healing we will attract the same issues over and over. We have to put the work in! When we really learn a lesson and are finished with it we never repeat it again.

A good example of this is when I was married I acquired a food addiction to comfort my pain and gained more than 100 pounds. I became an emotional eater. I lost 100 pounds during my ten months of therapy before I left my ex 28 years ago. I have worked hard to stay on a path of better physical health. Even with many emotional challenges since then I have kept that food addiction under control. I learned that lesson of how important it was to heal the inside back then and have never turned to binge eating again, even when life has been tough. The yoyo dieting stopped in 1997.

The lessons I have learned from my financial issues have been important. The last two months before I received my pension had been the most stressful financially. By then I had ran out of the money from the sale of my beloved suv. I had taken a portion of it to publish my last book, *The Married Man*, as well. Investing in my books is always worth it for me. Without taking risks there is no reward. I will always take risks to try and better my life.

By the end of summer 2021 and the last weeks before my pension kicked in I had nothing left to rely on. I had stretched every dollar as far as I could. I had dealt with the daily stress of not knowing how the heck I am going to pay my monthly bills and buy food for years by then. I made it through with some little and some big miracles. Saving $600 a month on my rent was pretty big and life changing. When I would relax and stop worrying things seem to suddenly flow into place for me. Yet, the closer I got to being one step away from being homeless the harder it became not to worry. That final stretch was a big challenge for me mentally. Wayne knew some of my financial struggles but I didn't tell him everything. I didn't want him to feel I was ever asking for a hand out.

I had done the work in cutting back on everything I possibly could in household bills. I had cut out the insurance payment on my suv as well by selling it. I called for my internet bill to be brought down to the minimum. I had gotten rid of my house phone two years before just to save ten dollars a month. Anything I could cut back on I did. I knew September and October 2021 were going to be the toughest months ahead and I also knew how it worked, the less I worried about it, help from God would show up in some form and I would be okay. Keeping my faith was everything to my survival because I was under enormous pressure!

Yes, I had taken some risks but never frivolous. I got through August only because I had sold my only nice ring I had left. I got less than half of what it was worth but it helped pay a bill and gave me enough to buy a gift and a cake for my daughters baby shower. This was important to me. I ran out of the money for food before I went into Edmonton for the actual baby shower. I was trying my best not to be tortured with worry every day. I worked through the worries with daily meditation and by staying aware as much as possible of how I was feeling.

If I felt sick to my stomach that meant I was worrying too much. I focused on feeling better by doing yoga, walking, reading, music, talking to family and friends and whatever it took to stay positive. Most of all keeping my faith and trust in God that this too would pass and all will be well. If I was complaining I would catch myself and put a stop to it. It did no good. I had to be grateful daily for the little things.

Dinah was driving to Edmonton the weekend of my daughters baby shower so it worked out perfectly that I could go with her and not have to take the bus which cost $210. I know there is nothing my friend wouldn't do to help me out but I struggled with asking her for anything. For the first time in my life I had to ask Dinah for $50 to buy some food while I was in Edmonton. Even though I had brought some food with me I knew I would need to buy extra for the few days I was there. (I am limited in what I can eat because of sensitivities so I always bring as much of my own food as possible.)

While we were driving I broke down and somehow found the strength and courage to ask her if she could loan me $50. It was indeed humiliating and I was certainly being humbled. She reached over right away and took my hand. "Yes of course luv, no problem." She said. I was so heart broken and very ashamed. My dearest friend pulled a $100 bill out of her purse and put it in my hand. I said "No, fifty is enough."

"Take it and don't worry about it." She said as she folded my hand over the bill.

"I'll pay you back." I replied wiping the tears that were now pouring down my face. It was pure agony for me to ask. Pure agony! Other than the loan from my sister when I bought my first rusty car more than two decades before this, I didn't ask anyone else to help me financially in my life. I tried giving her the other fifty back that I didn't use when we came back from the trip but she wouldn't take it. I always felt so much love from this woman and have never had anyone offer to help me so many times as she did during this time. I would always turn her down gracefully needing to keep my dignity and independence as much as possible and she understands that side of me. Many times she didn't listen to me and did what she wanted. Sometimes she would show up to visit with a bag filled with toilet paper, paper towel and a bottle of wine. *chuckles* It's the only times I would have a drink at home was with her. She is always giving, always kind and I am grateful to have her as a friend.

At a time when I was under tremendous pressure she was there checking on me constantly. With her there was no hesitating, no complaining, no questions asked just pure love and caring for me. Her heart is tremendous!

The race was on for my survival financially, now more than it had been in all my years, and that pressure was showing up a little more each day. I had to reach my goal to getting my OAP in October. The social assistance I received covered my rent and light bill for September month and that was it. I had nothing left for food or my other basic bills for the next two months. My credit card and line of credit had been used up for more than a year by then. If the internet was cut I would certainly survive but I needed food and to keep my apartment and my power on. These were the basics. With the price of groceries raising constantly in the past few years it would be a challenge. If the food bank was my next step I would have to take it.

I was well aware I had to stay positive, have faith and keep smiling. I knew staying happy as much as possible was the key to my survival. When my faith was strong I felt it. As the days turned into weeks I felt it more often than not. Positive attracts positive. Anything negative I was holding onto I would release at the very moment I became aware of it. If I ever got to that point again of thinking any dangerous thoughts I knew I would ask for help. I was very aware I was under tremendous pressure so I kept working on my passions daily that gave me some relief from the worry.

Again Dinah had offered to help those last months but I said I was okay at the moment and I would figure it out. "You would do it for anyone." She said, and she was right. I had helped many and continued to whenever I had an extra dollar, still, I couldn't bring myself to ask her for money again. I would never take advantage of anyone if I could figure it out myself. It gave me comfort just to know I always had her in my corner to help me if I needed it. I kept as much as I could about my worries from my children. As each day passed by the experience became even more humbling.

I sometimes thought of all the people that have had to ask for help in their lives. I had always been compassionate to those that suffer. This experience had made me became even more compassionate for others who struggle. By the end of this experience I finally allowed myself to feel some compassion for me and to not be as hard on me. I was learning to give me more grace. I was worth saving and I couldn't let this experience or any other take away from that confidant, courageous woman I had known over a lifetime now. I didn't allow me to forget I was worthy and worth fighting for.

One thing I have learned for certain about me, especially after going through four years of such a tough challenge financially, I never was and never will be comfortable being the taker but I know now if I need to ask for help I can do it more freely because I am worthy of help.

Thankfully I had received birthday money from my kids as gifts. That helped me get through September. My sons sent me more than we normally spend for birthdays and I was so grateful. I have good children. My daughter Hanna gave me a cell phone which I badly needed. The battery in my old one kept dying to the point I had to keep it plugged in to even use it. Jeanna gave me money as well. I paid for my internet and phone bill and kept what was left over for food. I left to walk to the grocery store with $70 dollars in my pocket for food for the rest of September month. I would get the very basics I needed.

Keep Going

Today I had a new experience for the very first time in my life. When the lady rang in my groceries I had to put two items back. I had gone over my limit. I felt the deep shame of it but brushed it off quickly and held my head up high keeping my dignity. It hurt my heart because I felt what many others feel daily in their lives. I lowered my voice and asked the cashier to take back the pumpkin seeds and chocolate bar. Two things I could live without. I felt tears welling up in my eyes and thanked God for the things I did buy. I told myself, "Just be grateful."

I handed the $70 to the cashier to pay for the bill that was $68.92. When she handed me the change I half smiled and said "thank you." I kept my head held high and walked out. I wiped away the few tears that escaped as I continued walking to the parking lot. As I left the store I thought about the times I would purchase six $25 gift cards at a time to just to hand out to customers at Walmart. I thought about how many times over my working years I had paid for people's items ahead of me, whether it was in a store line up or in a restaurant. I never questioned if they could afford it or not, I just loved helping people and hopefully making someone feel special. I had enjoyed helping the homeless in any way I could hundreds of times, when I worked and when I've been near broke, knowing one day this could be me. And here I was, for the first time putting things back. The shame only lasted a second. I shrugged it off. There could never be shame.

It's a killer! It could be far worse for me. I had to remember there are people dying in wars and starving to death every minute of every day. I was blessed and very lucky for all I had. I never stayed in self-pity asking "why me Lord?" Instead I said "why not me Lord?" I was determined to stay in gratefulness! Anything could happen at any given moment to bring us to our knees. God only knows I have been there over the years and He has shown up for me time and time again.

As I walked past a homeless man in the parking lot who asked for change, I literally gave him my last dollar. I was learning more and more that this kind of humility was to remember to still care for others and not to wallow in self-pity. Being grateful for the many blessings that did show up was key. Being ashamed that I had to put things back meant I was not being grateful in that moment for the things I did buy. I had to keep reminding myself not to go to the negative side.

People showed up for me in my time of need in different ways. God made sure of that. The most important thing was me showing up for me. I was definitely getting a taste of how close I had come to being homeless. I knew I wasn't too far from going to a shelter but I also knew I would do everything in my power not to. I felt a little broken in my heart but not in spirit!

During those trying times of giving up the man I loved and still keep the lights on I still made sure I put my lipstick on whenever I went out, even if it was just to take the garbage out and go for a walk. I put one foot in front of the other every day, holding my head high to remind myself of who I am and that I am not to be defeated! I don't walk in a slump of defeat, ever!

All the fears were there if I wanted to let them in but I was in survival mode! I knew I only had one month to go after this one and I felt some relief in knowing full well in my heart that I was being watched over and that things would show up to get me through the next month as well. My confidence was back! My bills had been paid for September and I had food to last a couple of more weeks if I stretched it.

The middle of October month Dinah offered to take me for groceries. I sucked it up and accepted her offer telling her I would pay her back as the tears fell. The tears were not because I was sad but because kindness makes me cry. I bought only what I absolutely needed that day and made it through October month. I tried paying her back when I did get the money but she refused to take it. This is why she and I have such a strong connection. We have the same heart when it comes to giving. I assured her I will pay it forward tenfold. When I did finally get my pension I took her out for supper and bought her flowers. Nothing big yet but heartfelt that I know she appreciated.

My Faith, a loving friend and my family who love me got me

through some of the hardest challenges of my life. The people I needed in my life to show up absolutely did.

Receiving my Old Age Pension and more than doubling my income gave me great relief! It was still poverty income by cost of living standards but it was a lot to me. I have learned to pinch pennies and don't need a lot to be happy. When that first OAP check came in I was cheering and dancing like a crazy person! Not only for the extra money but I was so grateful to still be here and become a senior! And of course as you already read I had also received the gift of my new granddaughter on my 65th birthday. There was so much to celebrate! Just months later I was moving in the right direction and healing more and more in moving on from Wayne. I felt much of that heavy cloud had finally lifted and I had made it! God is good!

Chapter 18

DESPAIR, REPAIR AND THE UNIVERSE

By the end of March 2022, I had a lot to be grateful for. I felt a shift happening in general and I felt myself coming back from much despair to a routine of positive energy flowing again. Covid 19 was becoming less threatening at this time as well and the world was opening up again. This was huge and so important for everyone's livelihood and mental health.

My family was doing well. My son Jeffrey had taken his first step in being part of a collaboration of authors in the books 'Business, Life and the Universe,' volume 5 and volume 6. He also has his own audible book released called Heaven to Hell by Jeffrey Saunders. I am so proud of all of his hard work. I don't doubt he will go even further on his journey in the world of healing and helping others. Jeff has taught me to have fewer fears of the unknown and to find my courage to try new things.

All of my children have taught me so much that I appreciate and am proud of. My son Jason has taught me patience, forgiveness and kindness. My daughter Jeanna has taught me strength, courage and acceptance. My daughter Hanna has taught me determination, compassion and the power of following our goals. They have all taught me to keep my humour and they all treat the homeless and vulnerable with great respect. They all have their mother's hearts.

I was now at a place where I felt I wanted to know more about what steps I should take next. This was now a time when I had hope again for something even brighter down the road. Some say we should not know what's coming down the road and to just live in the moment. That is wonderful and I agree. I also enjoy just getting a little glimpse now and then. I never put all my faith in it but I do enjoy getting a psychic reading once in a while from someone I feel is genuine. It has also helped me in the past to heal when getting messages from loved ones that have passed. It is always uplifting and a positive thing for me. I only deal with mediums that live their lives in light. I don't live in fear of mediums that are here to help with healing. Spiritual people don't live with all the fears that have been taught to us. Freedom without judgement of each other's beliefs is a must for me.

Being a Libra I struggle sometimes with making decisions but once my mind is made up I can act fast. Getting clarity and advice on decisions I am stuck on always helps. I was in a place where I needed guidance and I knew just the person who could help me.

Keep Going

I booked an appointment with my favourite and most trusted clairvoyant and medium Ginette Biro for March 15th 2022. Letting go of Wayne and then starting to get back on my feet financially was a wonderful feeling! I still missed Wayne and some days were still really hard but each day I grew stronger. Empowering as many people as I can especially young girls and women, from being abused and used by speaking about my own pain and in turn helping them to find their own strength and voice, means everything to me! It may take time to learn a lesson but there is always a way out for a healthier life, once we find our courage and strength. Dig deep! We all have it in us! And having struggles along the way to help build your worth and value internally will only make you stronger!

Over time with experience we see things more clearly. I suddenly had the realization one day that the men from my past had no God, no higher power in their lives to answer to. We all need someone to answer to. It keeps our integrity intact. This is what has been missing from all my romantic relationships in my life. I know now if I ever do fall in love again, it is important for me to find someone who is a believer. And like many times before after heartbreak and even at the age of 68, by the time I finish this book, I am keeping my heart and mind open for love again. I am forever a romantic. Having faith in God, Spirit, the Universe, Source, whatever you choose to call your higher power works for me. I don't want anyone radical and over the top for sure but if I do get involved with someone else he has to have faith in something higher than himself. This I am certain of. What an important lesson and awakening moment for me!

Chapter 19

THE READ

Ginette Biro is a beautiful and kind soul that my family and I have come to love, admire and respect. She has a book out called Avalon to Aurora. It is now on my top ten lists of favourite books to read. She is a clairvoyant and so much more. The handful of psychic reads I have had in the past have always uplifted me and have given me guidance. They have been 99% accurate. I choose wisely to who I trust in this area. Ginette is my number one choice.

It was the morning of my read and at 11 a.m. my phone rang and I answered. I was very excited to get any inspirational advice or messages from my loved ones who have crossed over as well. After a few minutes of chatting to this wonderful lady I filled Ginette in on what I was hoping for in the read. I had my questions ready and I had one hour to get as much information as I could. I am also a believer in that loved ones that have passed can help us here on earth with messages when we connect with good mediums. It can really be a wonderful and enlightening experience.

The first thing I asked Ginette about was moving. I explained to her that I was feeling pulled in two directions. Right away she said moving back to Edmonton would not be conducive for me and that the energy of living in Fort McMurray was better for me. I already knew I feel happier here in general. The atmosphere is more suited for me. It feels more like home. I had been torn because of my kids and some of my grandchildren being in Edmonton. Having my newest grandbaby was really pulling at my heartstrings. Hearing this from Ginette confirmed what I already felt. I already knew I didn't do well living in Edmonton. I just needed to hear it from someone else.

I love the surprises that come up in a read and this part of the read was the most important part for me that I want to share. I love when loved ones that have passed show up with messages that we need to hear in that moment.

I asked Ginette if any of my family were around. Right away she said, "Your sister is next to you. I saw a D name. She's been with you since before you wrote your first book."

I said, "Donna" as I smiled and teared up. "She's my soulmate."

Ginette said, "She has a message for you."

Donna said, "You are in the upswing. You can shift out of the doom and despair. Release all worries. We are co- creating what comes. Sit peacefully; I am always looking out for you. You are beginning a new chapter and I am your constant support."

Needless to say I was in tears… The message was just what I needed to hear. I couldn't have written a more beautiful and much needed message for myself if I tried. There is no doubt in my mind that Donna is aware of my struggles and is always looking out for me. I have felt my heavenly family helps guide me in creating my work as well. I feel inspirational writer's co-create with help from the Universe period. We are all connected as one.

I had been feeling things were finally turning around for me in the past weeks as I felt stronger and more myself than I had for quite a while. I had already released a lot of the negative I was struggling with in recent years and had made big decisions before the read. There was no doubt in my mind I was now on the right path and yes very much on the upswing as Donna had so gracefully put it.

I had asked about my health and Ginette gave me some good advice on making a few changes in food choices and on how to open up my lower chakras more. I am already doing this and energy wise it has helped me to feel better. I would go on to not only eat healthier but walk more and loose thirty- five pounds by the fall. Selling my suv that I had been so upset about had turned into a positive. I am learning more and more to not get upset about things out of my control and have faith that in time my perspective will change to see the positive in each lesson.

I had filled Ginette in on Wayne already so she knew some of the turmoil I had been in for the past few years. Even though some days I could still cry at the mention of his name, I felt I was finally in a good space of ending that for good. Ginette said, "Yes, that is over." I felt a sigh of relief. I went on to tell her that at this point in my life I would survive if I never found love again but I was still hopeful.

Ginette did tell me there was someone new coming. I did meet someone that fit the description she gave me but we have remained 'just friends,' nothing romantic for now. I was cautiously excited again to see what the future unfolds.

Ginette also touched on my debt that I had accumulated while living off my credit card and line of credit for those last years before my pension came. Never having debt before in my life this was still a burden I carried. She said there was money coming before Christmas to help me start paying it off. It would be a huge relief to me to pay off my debt completely. I just had to stay open and let it happen however it is meant to. At least now I had a timeline of it happening.

I did receive some money unexpectedly before and after Christmas in 2022. Not in the thousands but enough to get me started and in January of 2023 I did begin to pay off my debt. It has given me great relief to be able to start doing that. I am very grateful I had excellent credit my whole life and could use it at the time in my life when I needed it the most to help get me through a very difficult few years. It will take a few years to pay off but I have started rebuilding my credit again which has always been so important to me. By the time this book is released I am already half way there.

In the meantime I planned on staying in the 'upswing,' as my sister put it, every day as much as possible. That important and sweet message from Donna assured me I am on the right track. After the read with Ginette I felt even more optimistic for the future and was very happy to see some of the positive changes that followed.

Chapter 20

FORGIVENESS IS FREEDOM

Our journeys are our own to learn from and I learned a long time ago to choose and practice forgiveness over hate. Sometimes it might take some time in coming but it will always come when I am ready, not before. It is our own journeys to walk and it's up to each of us which path we choose. We can choose the path of resentments and bitterness or some people, the highly enlightened, can just let go in the moment and move on freely without carrying any pain in their heart. I have noticed in recent years I am not letting things get to me as much as I used to. I understand more about the reason we are here. I still work at it daily.

I have learned that any negativity others might throw at us can either be absorbed inside of us or can bounce off of us. Darkness can be rejected by our light. Whichever way we choose to receive or reject it will shape who we are. For me personally I choose to follow the path of freedom from all pain through forgiveness. It's a process for me to get there, depending on the offence. I work hard to always get there because that works best for me.

How do we forgive people who are narcissist that have hurt us deeply and has ripped our souls out and torn our lives apart to fulfill their own egos? It is not easy, especially if these people are our loved ones and we still have to interact with them. The truth is nobody has to forgive anyone and should not be pressured to or to be made to feel guilty if they make the choice not to forgive because the offence was so cruel. The main thing is we all have a choice and it is okay either way. I have always chosen forgiveness because it works best for me in my life to not hold onto pain and anger. I do it for me and my own health, no one else's.

When I was turning seventeen I was raped twice in a week. It happened the first time by a young man a couple years older than me and then the following weekend there was another young man a year older than me. They were related to each other. These young men had been friends of me and my sisters back then. We had gotten rides with them often from high school or dances, usually with groups of friends. The first man I was alone with for the first time had picked me up and was giving me a ride to my aunt's house. He pulled into a garbage dump and raped me. A week later the other man was giving me and my sister Donna a ride home from a dance and he dropped off my sister and took me parking. It was someone I really liked and had been out with once before. I had felt safe him so I was even more shocked and let down by what happened next. I had cared about him and I had every intention of telling him what had happened to me the week before but never got the chance. The minute we parked he got aggressive. I believe the first guy had told the second he had sex with me instead of telling the truth that he had actually raped me. I fought with each one but they were just too strong. I was held down and forced. I said NO to both men many times. Each time when I got home I went to bed feeling completely empty, alone and defeated. I didn't cry either time. I know I was in shock for some time after and couldn't understand why this was suddenly happening to me. I was not someone who was promiscuous.

Something had suddenly broke and changed inside of me. I walked around in a daze for some time after. Eventually I did cry and release some of the hurt about the second man because I had really liked him. I never dreamed he could hurt anyone. I grew to feel anger and distain for both men.

I was pretty mature for my age and knew enough that I couldn't let this ever happen to me again. I had to be more careful. One thing I had decided for certain was I was not going to let it break me because I had an awareness that it very well could have.

That summer I had worked my first job and had blossomed from a chubby girl to a slender young woman. I was on a high of feeling really good about how much better I felt physically. That soon changed and I felt horrible inside after the two rapes. I felt that I was suddenly a target. I learned a hard lesson back then of how I should not trust everyone. I told my closest friends and my sisters about the rapes but not my parents. The shame I carried back then was overwhelming! I did what most victims do; I blamed myself.

Two of my friends told me at the time that they had been attacked by one of the men before as well. It boggles my mind to think now of how many girls they may have actually raped in our community. It's never just one. I am sure we all blamed ourselves in some way because we all kept it between us. We were scared young girls. It was never our fault and they should never have gotten away with it.

Those incidents happening to me no doubt made me overprotective with my children and now grandchildren. They have certainly had an overload of talking to from me about safety. It was very different back in the seventies. My parents never spoke to us girls about any of this. It was the times we were living in and it was certainly not their fault. I could have turned to many bad things after that happened, like becoming promiscuous but I didn't. I still wanted love before sex and I am still that way. If I really like someone I will hold out for as long as it takes, which is not always easy for me. I am a true romantic at heart.

When I was in my early thirties and pregnant with my last child memories started bubbling up about the rapes that were causing me to be depressed. Things were coming up that I needed to deal with and could no longer bury. I wrote a letter to those two men that had raped me and then I burned it. I chose to release the pain and my own shame from those experiences. I gave it all back to them and I forgave them. I knew enough back in 1990 to know I didn't want what happened to me to continue to affect me or my family.

I carry absolutely no shame today and feel free and strong enough now to write about it openly. I forgave them for my own personal mental health, not theirs. It is the one thing I didn't write about in my book, *You Have to Go Now*. I wanted to protect my children. They know now and I have grown stronger. Speaking our truths without fear are the benefits and freedom of wisdom and aging. I really feel at this point in my life that the struggles that challenge us are not meant to break us but to strengthen us and our connection to self and God.

Helping others is my main focus now. Being open and speaking out is the only way to stop letting these perpetrators in the world win. Silence is their golden ticket to continue their behaviours. If calling them out is all I can do at this time in my life, at least it gives me and hopefully others some peace of mind because I know I am not alone. Just acknowledging it happened can be enough sometimes so we can finally take a deep breath again.

I had often wished I had the courage as a young girl to tell my parents and to have each of the men charged. I was scared and really felt if I did say something at the time it could be worse. I worried my dad might kill these men if he found out and he would end up in prison. All the fears and scary scenarios went through my brain back then. I can speak out about it now so young girls and woman are more careful in getting rides alone with men they think they know. More times than not I believe most attacks on women and some men are not done by strangers at all but by people we know. Forgiveness and letting go is the saving grace that I chose for me.

As we know fifty years ago rape wasn't taken serious many times in the courts and even today women are often not believed for these sexual assaults forced on them. It is a he said/she said situation that can often be hard to prove, especially years later. Date rape is the hardest to prove and it happens daily to many people. I at least can speak about it now so these men are not let off scot-free for their actions. I do believe justice will always prevail in one way or another either here or when we pass on. It is my opinion the more we heal the more peace we will feel while here and then in our passing as well.

It takes work to heal. For me it was first in writing the letter taking all the shame off me and forgiving each of them. I believe we can all find strength in each other by using our voices to speak up and be the survivors we are and to not spend our whole lives as victims. Moving from victim to survivor is so important to our self-worth. Even if it was decades ago, it matters.

There were two men in my teen years that I cared about enough to have sex with willingly. One was a crush and the other I felt I loved and I became pregnant for him at the age of eighteen. I had been seeing him off and on for a few years but never had sex with him until my eighteenth birthday. I became pregnant right away. The full story is in *You Have to Go Now*. I wore my heart on my sleeve and there is no doubt I was naïve. I really cared about him but because there was no commitment I moved on with my life. Other than those two men and those brief encounters there was no one else sexually before I met my ex-husband and I married three years later. I don't count the two rapes because for me it wasn't my choice.

There was one young man that I dated for a few weeks when I was seventeen that I did care about a lot and deserves mention. He treated me with so much respect and love. He never pressured me for sex. I believe now that after being raped just months before I started dating him that I didn't feel I deserved the kind of love he had offered me. I had felt damaged so I pushed him away not knowing how to handle genuine love. That and having feelings for someone else, that wasn't good for me in the end, speaks volumes that I didn't feel worthy of real love. It's taken me decades to figure this out. The good guy was protective and I know without a doubt loved me with his whole heart. He was tall, handsome and had a kind heart. I made him the love interest in my first novel When Lilacs Bloom. I'm truly sorry I hurt him. He deserved the best and I believe he has had a happy life. That makes me happy.

One thing I know for sure is that what happened in my past does not define who I am at my core. I can speak about it freely now to teach what worked for me. I want everyone to be free of pain before they die and to enjoy this life feeling lighter and happier through forgiveness, if they chose to. We all have lessons to learn. When we hit bottom and can rise back up is where real growth and strength happens. Our compassion and forgiveness for us and others becomes easier. When we can let it all go we have then risen to the top. Again, forgiveness is a choice. Speaking from my own experience, I highly recommend it.

It is also most important for me to say these three little words, I am sorry, if I hurt someone's feelings. I have always felt better after apologizing to someone if I feel I may have hurt their feelings. I am usually in tears because I genuinely feel bad about it if I made a mistake. It takes a lot of courage to face our errors. Most importantly it cleanses our soul and hopefully theirs too.

When it comes to friends, we all have lifetime friends and then we also have friends for a season that we learn from and have to let go of if our energy don't match. Most people I encounter treat me with love and kindness as I do them. Good friends are like gems, they are rare. Choose them wisely and hold onto them. The more I age the more I enjoy the company of making new friends. For a long time after losing my two sisters and two best friends in Edmonton I sheltered myself from making a lot of new friends because I feared the pain of losing anyone else. It took me a few years to realize what I was doing. I distanced myself for a while from getting too close to new people. Now I am back to enjoying my social life with a slew of new friends and I must say it's wonderful! I especially love my new friend Dorothy that I met last spring. Loyalty is everything to me and she is very loyal. We have fun and get along well. I call Dorothy, me and Dinah the 3 D's. *smiles*

When it comes to family I have forgiven close family that have hurt me in the past. Most of it with my family was with unhealthy addiction tendencies and behaviours. I have been taken advantage of and so have others in my family. That is continuous forgiveness until they are out of that environment of bad addiction because they repeat the same habits over and over. Eventually we learn to understand the behaviours more and judge less. We also have to stay strong and don't have to tolerate being taken advantage of. It's okay to say no and it's okay to walk away until they are well. Dealing with bad addictions with loved ones can literally tear a family or friendship apart. I have witnessed this too many times to count and wrote about it extensively in *You Have to Go Now*.

Try and forgive the antics. It is a disease.

I often watch real life crime shows because I enjoy seeing the bad guy/gal get caught and to see justice for families. Whenever I see a mother, father or any family member on a crime show find forgiveness for the person who harmed or killed their loved one it brings me to tears every time. I can only imagine the relief from the pain wrapped around their broken hearts. Although it is completely up to each person in whether they choose to forgive or not, I really believe their deceased family members would want that relief for them. I can only imagine it would be a nightmare to live through and can only imagine it would be the hardest acts to forgive. To see those families forgive the crime against their loved one is the most courageous thing I've ever witnessed. It is so wise and brave to relieve themselves from anger and bitterness. I admire these people so much!

They understand they could not rely on the justice system alone to give them the peace they need to be released from of pain, anger and hate. Only forgiveness could do that for them. We can all learn from these families that forgive the hardest things imaginable. Forgiveness is the best approach to even the worst situation in my opinion. I also understand and respect the people that choose to not forgive the worst crimes imaginable. They have every right to feel the way they do.

Through writing I found forgiveness for Wayne and Kitty back when I was ending it with him. I wrote him an email at the time expressing forgiveness for them both on behalf of me and my sisters. I know my heavenly family would want that. I also forgave me for not being strong enough to pull away once I knew the truth that he was married. I do feel in the deepest part of my heart, by the end of this whole scenario, they both lost far more than I did. She lost very good friends that loved her and he lost a woman that loved him beyond measure.

Forgiveness helped release the hurt. Writing this book has helped me tremendously. I feel by telling my story I am also helping a lot of people who have been stuck in similar affairs. It happened, it hurt and now I've healed. You can too.

People you choose to forgive don't ever need to know about your forgiveness in order for you to heal. This is a gift to you, not to them. You have the control. I promise you your heart will feel relief when you release pain and anger.

And remember the most important person to forgive for hurting others is you. No one is perfect. Shame is the worse invader and thief of our esteem. Let it all go!

I feel I am finally at a point in my life that if I should leave tomorrow I will leave in peace with no bitterness or carry any shame from past hardships in my heart. It may still take work sometimes as new things come up and that's okay. This path I'm on of freedom of all burdens and pain in my heart is important for me. At the end of every day I know I did my very best. That's all any of us can ask for.

It's taken me many decades to understand me more and to unscramble my past so I can be healthier today. Each relationship has been another step in this journey of learning what I want and don't want in my life. Each one has helped me build up my own worth to choose more wisely as to whom I let into my life, whether it's friends or a new love. My faith and loving number one on the inside is the most important thing in my life to work on for my true happiness. I do what I need to in getting here.

Finding forgiveness for all has been my saving grace to keeping an open heart to love and to not shut down. I know when we go through a lot that would be easy to do. I refuse to waste my life in bitterness. When we lose so many loved ones we learn that life is so precious and we should appreciate every breath of every day we get to still be here.

We have to allow feeling our suffering in order to heal our pain. Forgiveness really does lead to grace. Feel the freedom!

Chapter 21

THANKFUL FOR MY WORSE DAYS

It is January 28th, 2024. Today is a special day for me in writing this last chapter of this book. It has taken me two years to get here. The first 20 chapters flowed easy. I finished the first draft in 2 months and then nothing. I felt there was a reason I was stalled at what normally would flow and finish so easily for me. I would have to be patient to see if something would happen to inspire me to write an ending, or not. I did pick it up to work on the editing often. I would move sentences, paragraphs and chapters around and do my best to make it flow. Fixing and correcting errors in pretty much every sentence is a full time job. I am a terrible typist but I've learned to enjoy the process of editing. I think it's become a healthy addiction. I kept the faith that if this book was meant to be, the inspiration to finish it would eventually come to me.

And then this morning the flicker of an idea came to me. I suddenly wanted to finish with what I now consider the most important chapter in this book, which is having gratitude for my worse days. I feel this is such an important lesson for me to talk about and share.

How can we have gratitude for things that may have caused us stress or hurt us deeply you might ask? When I think about it the answer is not only in this book but is in every book I have written in some way. Without the hard lessons I wouldn't feel as strong, determined, disciplined or would I feel as whole and accomplished as I do in this very moment in my life. I am still here to co-create my own reality every day with guidance from above. I AM a part of a very big picture that we are all connected to and I AM the creator of my own story by my choices every day. The worse things that have happened in my life have without a doubt taught me the most.

Because I have the mentality, for many years now, of always being a survivor and not a victim has made me a stronger and healthier person both mentally and physically. I pull myself back up from the worse situations even when I have felt I just can't do it anymore. It could have very easily all gone another way for me many times with different choices, free will. I believe the choices I make in the end are the ones I am supposed to in order to learn each lesson. Sometimes those lessons get stuck on repeat for a while until I finally get it. I believe in the end the outcomes are the same because our paths are drawn out for us before we come here and even if we fall off that path by taking a different route (choice) we somehow end up back on track to the original plan, if that makes any sense?! It does to me.

Do I want bad things to happen? Certainly not! Who would?! I have to see the positives in the hard lessons because if I don't see life in general this way the bad can take me down and I'm not about to let that happen. So I wake up every day and appreciate the lessons learned. I'm still here and besides the fibromyalgia, which I am handling and keep improving, I can say I am healthier now than ever. That's a lot to be grateful for.

Being alone without a partner to lean on for most of my worse days has been hard for me. I don't have to be alone. It's my choice at the end of the day to be choosy. I do still get invites but none so far with anyone I feel pulled to explore. It's so important to know yourself and be true to you. The older I get the harder it has been to find a good man with integrity. I know there are some out there. I just haven't met the right one for me yet. I know me well enough to know I would not be happy at all settling, just to have a partner. Any of us can do that any day of the week. I don't settle. That all important emotional connection that is so rare is still a must for me even if the looks are fading with age for many of us.

It would be great to have someone to talk to about the day's events and to have a shoulder to lean on on my worse days. I am at a point now where I don't need to live with anyone but to have a loyal and devoted partner that I could trust and that lived close by would be wonderful. In my opinion life is meant to be shared with someone we love. We all want a witness to our life and to share our stories with along the way. To have someone I could fall into the arms of when my world has been turned upside down would be so wonderful and comforting. Will I survive without it? Definitely! I already have.

On the other hand, if I had a full time partner over the past twelve years I may have been too busy and distracted to focus on writing at all. I was certainly distracted by *The Married Man* but at least by the end of that chapter I can say I turned that heartache into something positive, a fictional novel that I love and will be around for people to enjoy hopefully long after I have passed on. And now to tell the whole true story so others can maybe learn and heal from a similar situation is very rewarding for me. We meet everyone in our lives for a purpose or a reason. I can't say that enough because it is so true. From the feedback I received, *The Married Man* touched other people's hearts. That is the positive side that comes from healing through art.

Some of the most profound and beautiful creations put out by artists in many forms often stem from heartbreak while going through our worse times. Art helps release pain, to feel joy and whatever other emotion of the day we might be having. We can turn the worse things that happen to us into something healing, amazing and hopefully lasting.

This has been all important work for me to grow and learn

more about me so I can be a better human being and partner if I were blessed enough to find someone special. I feel at my age now with so much more knowledge that this would be the best time for me to fall in love again. I can honestly say I still believe in love and I have learned so much I am more equipped to make better choices. I also know that the most important person on this planet who can care for and love me is me.

Taking risks is very important. I have taken many over the years and I'm so happy I did whether they pan out or not. There are times I've went beyond my means to take a risk. Nobody would be doing extremely well in this world that didn't take risks at something they felt passionate about. If we fall, we get back on the horse. Some become rich and famous from it, others like me just enjoy the process with no expectations. That is the key to staying young at heart. Doing what we love is the most important good karma in life. There is no such thing as failure as long as we try and we enjoy the journey of our passions. The more I learn to live in the moment the more God will bring me what I need.

Even at 68 by the time I publish this book, I still feel forty in my brain and heart. The physical aging and looks have defiantly changed and as depressing as some of it can be I embrace it all. I've earned every line and wrinkle. I will hopefully stay around another 20 or 30 years, God willing. I still have a lot to do. I have always wanted to do my own album of songs one day for my own satisfaction and something to leave my family. My voice is still pretty strong.

I would enjoy my own little home with a washer and dryer of my own. Apartment life is okay but not my dream place for sure. What is life without a dream?! If the day comes when I no longer have a good quality life I would be fine going to join my heavenly family whenever God sees fit. Life is a cycle. We have to make the best of every moment we are here today.

I have learned I don't need to figure out why things are happening the way they do as much as I used to. Although I will always have a curious nature I just have to trust there is a reason or purpose and that in the end the worse things often turn into the best things for us to learn from and to help us lead better lives. We just have to be aware enough to see the benefits of each lesson.

Spiritually I know I am never alone. He has always been there for me and will never leave me. I feel that more strongly now than ever.

Being a senior for me brings with it even more freedom of being able to talk openly without fear. I was so fearful when I put out my first book of being criticized and judged. Now I don't care what the heck anyone thinks. I feel that comes with age and experience. I've learned that having grace for me and others is freeing. Letting go has helped me feel free and happier inside. I have heard that seniors have no filter and I am certainly more outspoken. I'm not sure if that is always good, especially on a Saturday night after a glass of wine. *chuckle*

Each experience has been a stepping stone to building a stronger, more resilient and hopefully wiser us as a whole, as we age. Not all of us become wiser with aging. There are some human beings that never learn because they are stuck living in a toxic world of addiction. Pray for them to find courage and strength. I'm not here to judge and as sad as it might be for me knowing this about people I love I will continue to love them. As some of us that have been through the wringer know that is not always easy to do. We do our very best and believe it or not, they do too.

The worries about my financial woes were some of the worse days of my life. It was the heaviest burden and one of the most challenging for me to carry. I am thankful for that very hard lesson now because I have learned to be humble in an entirely new way. It is hard to be grateful when we are in our worse days but once it passes us hopefully we will see the true value of the experience. The humility of having to ask for help in my darkest times didn't come easy for me but it made me more human and less above it all. It humbled me. I had no problem reaching out and asking for therapy or other ways of helping and healing me and my family in the past. That was much different in my view than asking for a hand out. I see things in a whole new light now that I have given myself grace. I see it as courageous and admirable to reach out and ask for help instead of shameful, as long as we are not taking advantage of people's good hearts. I see the blessing now of being brought to my knees and asking for help.

Sharing my own experience with you will hopefully help some people to be more compassionate toward the homeless. It could be any of us when life suddenly sends us a curve ball with our health or in many other ways. A big positive that came out of my financial struggle was selling my suv which forced me to walk more and in turn has made me healthier. Getting in better shape is definitely a blessing for me in my mobility and the daily pain I suffered from. It's amazing what blessings can show up from many of our dark times once we get through them and can look back and see the actual light that came out of the experience. I do know with struggle comes strength.

Without the worse days of my life what would I have learned? Absolutely nothing! Would I do it all again? I would say yes because I believe I am meant to learn more about me than about anyone else in my journey here. I did experience the excitement of new romantic love in my life a few times even when it didn't work out and couldn't last forever. I have experienced many years of true happiness and as I have healed through the worse times I still believe that the best times are here today and yet to come.

Joyful times are great! They are the best experience and place we all want to be. For the majority it is not our realities all the time. We don't learn a lot of lessons of lessons from the joyful times, we simply enjoy them. It is in those joyful times when we live fully in the moment. We all want and work towards more of that. Whether we get what we want depends on us following our passions. The more joyful we are daily in doing what we love the more joy we will create and attract. I have learned one clear lesson for sure and that is that worrying does nothing but steal our joy.

Our worse days are where our most valuable lessons come from that teach us to do better the next time. I would hate to wake up at my age now and know I didn't have any failures because I never tried the things I feared. I have walked through a thousand fears, some successfully, some not. The most important thing is to try.

Material happiness is fleeting. We can make anything look good on the outside and that is important to a point to feel good temporarily but it is healing the inside that really matters to feel truly happy. That is success to me.

I Keep Going not only for me but for my children and grandchildren and most of all for God. He gave me life and wants me to live my best life. I know He watches over me, protects me and guides me. Although some days are still going to be a challenge I know with His love and guidance I got this!

Keep Going

I remember that little seven year old girl in the middle of her nanny's kitchen fondly and with so much love. How much she has gone through and how far she has come standing strong so many times in life with help from God and the people that love her. I am certain she would choose to go through her worse days again because the woman she has become is stronger for it. Her strength and purpose is to help as many people as she can by telling her own story with courage, honestly and absolutely no shame. When I picture her now her head is not bowed downwards, her head is held high while still wearing her tender heart open and on her sleeve. I love her profoundly. She has not wasted her life experiences and has grown to help others any way she can, even by exposing her deepest, darkest secrets.

We can all council and help each other through sharing our own experiences. We don't need a degree for that, just courage. If nothing else I want my story to empower other women and men to find their own voice as well.

Keep Going!

Chapter 22

WE LOVE YOU MACKENZIE

In this journey called life we never know what's coming around the corner. Just weeks after finishing what I thought was the last chapter of this book about learning from my worse days, I never expected the absolute WORST day of my life was about to happen. I need His strength and guidance now more than ever to lead me in the words I'm about to write.

I am grateful for experiencing the love of my granddaughter for twenty years. I know there are grandparents that don't get to experience this life with a grandchild for more than a day or a week sometimes. In this very moment as I write, losing my beautiful granddaughter is still inconceivable to my heart!

Nothing can prepare us for the tragedies that can bring us to our knees. I have prayed to God many times now after losing many family members and friends to please not take my grandchildren or children as long as I am still alive. It was arrogant of me to think I have that kind of control. With all that's happened in my life that I had already lived I didn't feel

I would be able to ever survive such a great loss as a child or grandchild and here I am...I feel this is very important to write about. Far too many of our children are dying from suicide.

On April 9th 2024 I was out for my daily walk. Even though it was a cloudy and windy day I was enjoying it. When I arrived back home around 3 pm and as I was walking on the sidewalk leading into my apartment building, I looked down and low and behold directly in front of me there was a beautiful deep orange and black monarch butterfly sitting in the center of the walkway. I found it odd because it was still quite chilly outside. I had yet to see any other sign of any kind of insect life in this early spring. It stopped me in my tracks!

My granddaughter MacKenzie came to my mind right away. We have a photo of Kenzie's hand that she took when she was camping a few years before with an orange and black butterfly and a dragon fly sitting on her hand. I assumed that's why she came to mind in that moment. Creatures big and small were drawn to her.

(Many other times in my life I received premonitions and signs from loved ones who were passing or about to pass without me knowing it until later.)

I looked down and talked to this butterfly as I watched it lift its wings sporadically and then rest them again. It captured my full attention. It was so beautiful. It just sat there peacefully while dead leaves flew past us from the wind. I couldn't help but watch in amazement that the wind didn't seem to make any difference to this tiny creature's stance. I whispered "Where did you come from and what are you doing here little butterfly?" After a few minutes of taking in its beauty I left it alone praying it would not be harmed. I didn't know until later that the butterfly is also the sign of hope for suicide victims. Its meaning is the progression from a cocoon of internal struggles of mental health into a beautiful winged butterfly. I believe now this beautiful sign that showed up in my path that day was a sign from my granddaughter MacKenzie that she was leaving us to be in the spirit world.

Two hours later at 5:15 my phone rang but I didn't hear it. At 5:27 it rang again. I picked it up and said "hello." When my daughter Jeanna spoke she was clearly in distress and was crying. It was a sound I always dread hearing from my children because I know something bad has happened. I froze and I listened! "Mom where have you been?? I called you ten minutes ago and you didn't answer!!" She cried.

"I was outside walking but have been home since three. I didn't hear the phone. What's wrong??" I asked, staying as calm as I could as my heart raced and my whole body started to tense up!

"The nurse called me from the hospital and Kenzie tried hanging herself with a sheet in a bathroom! They couldn't get her pulse for 11 minutes! She's on life support!!" She cried.

Keep Going

"WHAT??!! OMG!!" I felt my legs go weak!

"Can you go to the hospital to be with her Mom??!!" She begged.

"YES, I'll find a way there and go!!" I cried.

Jeanna said she was getting ready to leave and drive here. As I hung up I felt fear fill my mind and body as I tried to think straight of what to do next! This was my daughter and granddaughter. I had to keep it together!

To see my granddaughter like this would be devastating and I was scared I couldn't handle it but I had to do it! My children live more than a four hour drive away in Edmonton so it would be awhile before I had my family here with me.

I picked up my phone to call my friend Dinah who was luckily on her way home from work. After I tearfully blurted out what Jeanna had told me she said "I'll be there to get you in fifteen minutes!" Dinah was as loving and compassionate as always telling me not to worry and she was here for me. I rushed around to get ready and then made my way downstairs to where Dinah was waiting for me.

By the time we got to the emergency Kenzie's dad was already there waiting for news. My ex-husband, Kenzie's grandfather, showed up soon after as well. We were all anxiously waiting in a tiny room about thirty minutes before the emergency room doctor came in to speak to us. As he explained the situation to us I picked up on an inaccuracy in the story. He said they found my granddaughter at around 1:30 pm and they had to resuscitate her. She was now intubated. I questioned the error in his information he was giving us. I knew that time he gave us was impossible because Kenzie had been online chatting in our group messenger. Her last message sent to us was at 3:28 pm. I had the text. There was no indication in the text that Kenzie was going to harm herself. The Doctor didn't know what to say other than they were estimating the time. Really? That was at least a two hour mistake. He went on to say that nobody on the mental health ward had seen Kenzie for 35 minutes before someone looked and found her in the bathroom. My mind was blown as my heart broke into!

My granddaughter had gone there for help like she did many times before when her mental health wasn't good. She would go there to feel safe.

A little while later Kenzie's psychiatrist came to speak to us briefly. He told us MacKenzie was suicidal when she went there looking for help. When she wanted to leave he had told her no and admitted her. He told her he was keeping her there for thirty days. Normally if she was suicidal and was admitted they would have had someone shadowing her to make sure she didn't harm herself until she was stable. We don't know enough yet to speak on why there was no one with her that day or why no one had checked on her for that long.

After the doctor left the nurse came in the room and told us we could see MacKenzie if we wanted to. As much as I didn't want to see my granddaughter on life support I gathered up my strength and my wobbly legs and followed the nurse. Everyone else followed into the ICU.

I have no words to describe seeing my beautiful twenty year old, smart, articulate, funny, quirky, sarcastic and now broken granddaughter with tubes and machines inside and around her, other than f**king devastating!! My heart shattered into a million pieces as my legs felt like they were going out in under me! Dinah squeezed my hand tight and stayed next to me holding me up.

I was filled with instant heartbreak, compassion, anger, grief and sorrow!! I told myself to breathe and keep it together as I took Kenzie's hand carefully that had an IV attached to it. I talked to her through tears with words of comfort and to let her know I was there. "Nannies here sweetheart. I love you." I whispered as tears poured and the helplessness set in. Her grandfather was across the bed from me and he was in tears and was holding her other hand. Her father had left the room. He later told my daughter it was too much for him seeing her that way. It was a lot to take in.

My two daughters Jeanna and Hanna, Jeanna's partner Steven

and my 13 year old granddaughter Sofia (Kenzie's sister) arrived from Edmonton later that evening. It was painful to see my daughter's heartbreak when she saw her child lying lifeless in a vegetative state. Jeanna stayed calm as she tended to and talked to Kenzie in a soft and gentle voice. She touched her carefully and tenderly as tears poured quietly. I wished it was me lying there in my granddaughters place. How unfair this was to my granddaughter in being so young. She didn't deserve this!

The very next day it was decided by the staff to fly MacKenzie to Edmonton to the University Hospital for better care than they had available here in Fort McMurray. We all packed up and went to Edmonton for the next eight days and nights to face some of the hardest and worst days of our lives as a family. I was extremely worried about Jeanna as well. Her being the mom I knew this was a hundred times harder for her.

We arrived at Hanna's home near Gibbons before we left to drive to the University hospital. Hanna had been texting with Jeanna who had already arrived at the hospital. Hanna showed me a text that Jeanna sent her. It simply said, "I need Mom." I couldn't get there fast enough!

When we all met up at the hospital I hugged Jeanna tight and tried to prepare myself to face whatever was ahead. I can't tell you the roller coaster ride we were on not knowing from one day to the next if Kenzie would survive. There had been no change and by some of the comments my family was over hearing from the nurses I can tell you it didn't look good. By day six we did have a glimmer of hope because we were told they still didn't have any solid answers yet but they would reassess her in two weeks. They also said they were moving her to another floor in a bigger room with big windows. Great! We all needed more light for sure and it gave me great hope and relief that at least Kenzie wasn't going anywhere any day soon.

We were all with her daily. Her mom and step dad Steven would stay until later in the night. My granddaughter and my daughter were on my mind constantly. Jeanna had struggles with her own mental health in the past. She has done a lot of work to help herself but this was a lot for anyone to take on. I can only imagine the pain, agony and helplessness she felt.

Jeanna was at Kenzies bedside the whole time taking care of her. I knew she was barely keeping it together but she did. Her strength was incredible! I give her a lot of credit and I am very proud of her. She stayed stronger than the rest of us most of the time. My son Jeffrey was also there on those last days with us and I am grateful for the work he did at home and at the hospital to help Kenzie spiritually in her last days.

Because the doctor had said they couldn't do anything more for two weeks my ex and I decided to come back to Fort McMurray to try and rest up, collect some more things we needed and then head back to Edmonton again. We had planned to go back to the hospital the next day to see Kenzie one more time before we left.

When my ex and I walked into Kenzie's new room the next day Jeanna was standing there with a doctor I had not seen before. He was standing across the bed from her. Kenzie's father and her other grandfather had just left. Jeanna turned and looked at me as I stood close to her. I could see she was physically shaky and she had tears in her eyes. Then she spoke, "There's nothing else they can do. They are taking her off life support on Thursday. This gives family time to say goodbye." I realized later how hard that must have been for her preparing to share such devastating news to those of us who loved Kenzie and her so much!

"What? OH NO!!" I cried! "This can't be happening!" I was in disbelief!! We knew this was possible but we had gotten a glimmer of hope and now there was suddenly none?! (They had done an MRI and that's why I believe the doctors had now come to this conclusion of no hope. I also now feel this was why Kenzie was sent to this floor to pass peacefully with her family around her.)

Jeanna and Kenzie's dad had already made the decision days before that they would not leave their daughter to live in a vegetative state forever and we all agreed, never wanting to believe it would come to that. And now here we were as deep sadness filled the room.

We stood there weeping as I put my arms around my daughter. Jeanna had been so strong. She would cry quietly but still kept it together. I pulled it together and did my best to do the same for her. Although she was showing so much strength I knew she was fighting hard not to fall apart. She was on a mission to take care of Kenzie until the very end and she did. I watched as the whole family wept openly in the next hours and days. My son Jeffrey laid his head on Kenzie before he left and wept like a baby as I stood next to him and rubbed and kissed his head. Hanna fell apart in the waiting area as we sat next to each other. She laid her head on my lap and I held her and let her cry it out.

MacKenzie's parents, grandparents, Uncles and Aunts, my son in laws, Kenzies cousins and her boyfriend who were there, all wept openly. We all loved MacKenzie with our whole hearts!

And now with all of this anguish inside our hearts and souls, decisions had to be made whether we liked it or not. I stayed out of all decision making unless I was asked. I was there to help in any way I could and to support.

I was glad Jeanna and Kenzie's dad had decided to bring in a minister to pray over Kenzie and to pray with us. The next day the Anglican minister came to anoint Kenzie and she said a prayer. She was very kind and compassionate.

On April 18th my daughters Jeanna and Hanna, Kenzies dad,

the two grandfathers and me surrounded my beautiful granddaughter's bed. The rest of the extended family and her boyfriend had already seen her to say their goodbye's right before this. Most of them had stayed and were still outside waiting in the waiting area.

Just after 12 pm the doctor and nurses, who were very compassionate and loving, removed the machine that had been helping Kenzie breathe. Kenzie had always said she wanted to donate her organs and so her wish was being granted. There was a team quietly waiting outside her room to take her to surgery five minutes after her final breath and heartbeat. The doctor made it clear several times that Mackenzie's comfort came first before anything and she would be treated with the upmost respect during surgery. This gave us comfort.

We loved on Kenzie, touched her, held her hands and talked to her with words of love and compassion and with so much deep heart wrenching sadness! My daughter made me proud in her strength and yet tore my heart out to see her stay so strong while the tears still flowed as she continued loving on her daughter. I couldn't bear to get the words out but I hummed the hymm Jesus Loves Me to our sweet Kenzie as we watched and waited dreading the inevitable that was now happening in front of us. Jeanna lay her head on Kenzie's belly and was whispering "It's okay, it's okay." Later on she stated that she wasn't sure if she was saying it to Kenzie or herself. My feeling is she was saying it to both. A mom and child being torn apart; there is nothing more painful in life! I felt the floating feeling hitting me. That all too familiar feeling of grief from my past losses. Familiarity doesn't make it easier, just more aware.

Mackenzie took her last breath peacefully at approximately 1:19 pm. We all kissed her and said I love you as we stood back quietly and waited the five minutes. Nobody spoke a word. We would glance at the monitors where there was just a slight blip from her heartbeat as my granddaughter left our world and into the next to be with her past loved ones. I believe with all my heart they were also there standing by the whole time to take care of her, guide her and to take her spirit home.

For us left behind it is another story. We have to carry and bear the pain and suffering of missing her. I thought I would faint as my legs became numb underneath me.

The doctor and the nurses came in a few times and were checking things while quietly giving their condolences to us and leaving again quickly to give us space. For reasons I am not clear on yet we were not allowed to touch her and had to stay back after her last breath. I wasn't there when that part was explained. I believe it may have been to clear the way for the team that was taking her to surgery.

When the five minutes passed the team that had been quietly and respectfully waiting outside in the hallway came in and quickly prepped and wheeled Kenzie's bed from the room. Hanna and I called out "We love you MacKenzie!" I knew Jeanna couldn't speak.

When I looked at Jeanna, my Molly (her nic name), standing next to me I could clearly see she was finally letting go of all she had held back in those nine long days. She was breaking down. Her body was shaking and trembling as her sister wrapped her arms around her and I wrapped my arms around them and Kenzies dad and the two grandfathers wrapped their arms around us. We all cried and held Jeanna up to help her while she released that guttural cry that only a wounded mother losing her child could cry. It was the most heart wrenching and painful sound and experience of my life!

Our jobs now would be to survive this as a family while supporting each other daily. Thank God for one thing, my family and I have learned many coping skills from therapy over the years. We have to dig deep and use them wisely to survive this tragedy and in our hearts and minds, a great injustice on many levels. My daughter and Kenzie's father are left to suffer more than I can imagine. I only wish I could take away their pain. All I can do is my best to help any way I can and to love my daughter through it. I had to make sure this didn't kill us too! I believe with all my heart and soul she will survive and live her best life for her and for Kenzie. I believe Kenzie will make sure her mom is okay as she now watches over her and all the people and pets that she loved with all her heart.

Keep Going

I never expected that this book would end in such a heartbreaking way. I have written about my survival and so many of the lessons I have learned so far. I have done so much work to Keep Going and to enjoy the little things in life as much as possible. I will do my very best to continue to do that for my granddaughter and to make her proud as she made me proud in all of her accomplishments and for her huge heart. We are all fighters in this journey called life. My granddaughter fought hard too. As much as Kenzie fought in the end she lost her will to live. Something she was working hard not to do. I know if she was her true self she would never have harmed herself this way. Sometimes to Keep Going is just too hard for some like my granddaughter. Considering the circumstances she was under I Know Mackenzie did her very best! Mackenzie captured all of our hearts forever and always. We love you sweetheart!

Chapter 23

MENTAL HEALTH AWARENESS

MacKenzie had some mental health issues since she was a young child but nothing compared to her last three years after she had been diagnosed with several mental health issues and put on multiple, mental health medications. She always had control of not acting on her thoughts. After she was put on the medications at the age of seventeen she started to often lose that control. Kenzie started to change in both her looks and personality while on these medications prescribed by her doctor. I could still see the sweet side of our beautiful Kenzie but she was never the same for most of the last three years of her life. She became darker in her attitude towards herself and life in general. I have photos of her before and after she was medicated that are all telling.

I will give my opinion of some of the things that I feel contributed to bringing my granddaughter to this tragic point in her life so that just maybe someone will read something that connects with them or a family member. It might help save a life. Just maybe something good could come from something tragic, as it often does.

I don't have any kind of degree in psychology but I have learned a lot by reading about other people's journeys, my own life journey of having dealt with anxiety and watching other people's behaviours that I personally know that have dealt with mental health issues. Sometimes having life experience can teach us more than any classroom. Life is a school in itself. Please consult your doctors on any decisions in dealing with any mental health issues. If you don't feel comfortable with one doctor, find another one. Most are good but they are not all the same.

I have nothing against taking medications. They are very important and help a lot of people. I believe medications do work when a patient is diagnosed properly and prescribed medication properly.

My youngest daughter dealt with post-partum depression and had to go on a medication that helped her. One didn't work so her doctor tried another and it did work. It got her through some tough months until she didn't need it anymore and she weaned herself off them safely. For that I am grateful. It is very important to wean yourself off any mental health medications. From what I have learned it can be dangerous to just stop taking them. Follow your doctor's advice in doing that.

It is of my opinion that too many young people and adults with mental health issues are walking around in a daze being over medicated. How could they possibly think clearly when taking many mind altering medications at once and then having to deal with all the side effects from them? Taking 8 or 10 medications a day like my granddaughter was prescribed, in my opinion, only messed her up more. There are some doctors that will prescribe a handful of meds to you right away when you see them with mental health issues. In my opinion it is a red flag. We have to be aware of this.

Both my daughter Jeanna and my granddaughter Kenzie went through trauma as young girls. I am a believer in deep therapy and coping programs to help heal the effects of trauma. Jeanna was also diagnosed with multiple mental health issues and put on multiple medications right away after going for professional help 10 years ago when she felt she needed help. She weaned herself off all of them within 4 months because she felt she was doing way worse and was actually going crazy on the medications. I can only imagine that my granddaughter felt even worse considering she was prescribed twice as many as my daughter had been taking back then. I was very upset about it with both of them being on so many medications and made it clear to each of them how I felt. I knew my words only went so far.

Thankfully Jeanna was old enough in her late twenties and clear minded enough to be aware and figure it out. As she weaned off the meds she got into programs and therapy that in her case helped her more. She felt the medications were doing her more harm than good. Jeanna did the work in

Keep Going

figuring herself out by research and discovered she has DID (dissociative identity disorder). She is doing amazingly well now since she took the programs to learn about it and to learn coping skills. I'm really proud of her and I lovingly call her my chameleon. Not every person has the wherewithal to do this work, especially young teenagers like my granddaughter. So many depend so much on finding proper medical help.

Kenzie was so young at seventeen when she was first diagnosed and medicated. A teenager's brain isn't even developed enough to figure out or even know what is happening to them. She also trusted her doctor completely as most people would because he is a 'doctor' and did what he told her no matter how much we, her family, questioned it and fought with her and her doctor about some choices that were made. My family knows how I feel about taking medications if it is avoidable and when there are healthier options. I have been on their last nerve many times I am sure. Mackenzie said to me several times when I would openly worry and ask questions about what she was taking, "I don't want to hear anything about meds Nanny." I would pull back not wanting to make her angry and now feel I should have screamed it louder.

I do know that for the first 17 years of MacKenzie's life she never had any suicide attempts or admissions to hospitals for her mental health. The mental health issues she did have she never acted on to attempt suicide. Since she had been put on the multiple medications when she was 17, she was admitted to different hospitals more than fifty times in three years for mental health issues. She went many more times when she wasn't admitted. They even did shock treatments for days at a time on her twice while she was in a hospital in Edmonton. She was kept in hospitals for weeks at a time. All of those times she was admitted in the past three years were because she was having mental break downs and some were suicide attempts. You can draw your own conclusions from these facts as I have.

I have often wondered how many of the kids committing suicide in recent years, since the numbers have gone way up, have been highly medicated? I don't have the skills or means to find this out but I pray someone that does would look into it. I do know just one of the drugs that Kenzie was taking was Abilify, which from what I read can have extreme side effects. I have tried to get a list of the other medications with no success yet. I know she was taking them pre-packaged twice a day. Each pack had 4 or 5 pills.

MacKenzie became more aware and afraid of all the side effects from the medications. There were so many. She was having heart palpitations and she had started having seizures that last year. One time she drank alcohol while on the meds. She learned a hard lesson from that and didn't do it again. She had another seizure while on her break at work while out shopping. An ambulance was called. I know it really scared her and made her have even worse anxiety! She felt faint often. She had developed very low blood pressure. She would throw up for no reason, often with blood in it. Her lips would turn purple sometimes. There were no real answers as to why all of this was happening to her from her doctors but my instincts always told me it was side effects from all the medications. She never had any of these things happen to her before taking the meds. Her moods were constantly changing and often she could be very dark in her attitude and humour.

It was very hard to have my hands tied. I often wished I could take her to a cottage near a lake, away from everything and everyone and just take care of her myself. I would tell her that and she would say, "I would love that Nanny." If I had the means to do it she knew it would definitely have happened. She had also agreed she would have gone to a treatment center in BC that we researched and found out was having good results in helping people. If I had the $30,000 to send her she would have went. Unfortunately we all don't have that kind of money.

I will make some suggestions that might help some mental health issues in some cases, especially for anxiety. This is coming from my own experience having dealt with agoraphobia for many years. Again, I'm no doctor and I know medications are needed to help many patients and they do. It's the overload of meds that in my families experience do more harm than good. I also believe there are other tools that can be used in some cases that don't need medications but maybe some different knowledge in other areas.

Sometimes I suggested doing meditation that I felt could help Kenzie tremendously but getting her to try it was not easy. How could anything be easy for her when she couldn't think straight most of the time?! She did agree to try an energy healing technique that I use for my fibromyalgia and any other health issue I may be dealing with. She had a wonderful experience. I think she was surprised by it. I did see a positive change in her right after and I was happy she at least tried it. She drew pictures of her experience and sent them to me right after. She also posted a new profile photo that same day on her social media. I could see a twinkle and some light back in her eyes. It was amazing to see! This was just a few months before her passing. I was so proud of her for trying something different. I tried to encourage her to continue the practice but that was not to be her journey.

Kenzie had weaned herself off all medications two to three months before she had her last meltdown, except for the shot of Abilify she was still taking once a month. She didn't tell me she was weaning herself off the medications until she was a few weeks in. I asked her about it because I had noticed she was less irritable and was suddenly taking on more shifts at work because her anxiety was far better. She was pleasant and seemed to smile more and was happier in general. She wasn't cutting herself anymore which was something she did often before that.

I don't know what brought on her melt down that last day she went for help. I do know because she was talking of hurting herself again so her doctor admitted her for 30 days and put her back on the medications she had worked so hard to come off of. I can only imagine how she felt in those last days she was in the hospital in lock down again. I can't bring myself to think about it but she had clearly felt defeated and had enough.

Something else to watch for in young girls and women that have mental health issues is serious premenstrual syndrome. Kenzie would often have bad anxiety many times brought on by her period which could lead her into full blown panic attacks. Her periods had gotten dangerously heavier and more frequent in the last year as well. I believe another side effect from the medications.

My opinion is based upon my talking to Kenzie almost daily, many times 2 or 3 times a day. If I didn't hear from her I instinctively knew she was back in the hospital. I watched her, asked questions and kept track of her mood swings. I talked to her often about talking to her doctors and trying different hormonal treatments instead of all the medications she was on. I don't think anyone took her PMS serious enough.

We need to pay more attention to the connection with hormones and mental health in women. Low estrogen can cause mood swings, sadness, nervousness, irritability, anxiety, frustration and a skin crawling sensation. Kenzie definitely experienced all of those symptoms when it was her time of the month. When kids are sensitive and don't understand what they are feeling, anxiety can build to fear and turn into full blown panic. PMS is something to seriously look at and to keep in mind for young girls and women suffering with depression and/or anxiety. It took me years as a young woman to figure out what was happening to me when I started having PMS. I can't imagine taking many mind altering mediations on top of this?! I don't think I would have survived it.

It is also my opinion we need more spiritual people working in the mental health system. We need experienced people that practice medium ship and have clairvoyant skills that can help others that are gifted to take their fears and anxieties away by teaching them how to handle their own gifts properly. Spiritual healers are becoming more open now in helping and giving advice in teaching others who can see spirits and don't know what the heck is going on with them. Especially children who are taught to be fearful because no one believes them and would rather diagnose them as crazy and put them on meds right away. This is so wrong. We as a society need to be more open to this being a natural gift for many and not a mental illness. I truly believe it could save lives if the medical world would open up more and get past the fears of the unknown because of beliefs that are old school. I believe this tool of having experienced people work in this area could really benefit the mental health system. Open up scientist! You don't know it all!

There are sensitive, intuitive, spiritual people that really do hear and see dead people and it is okay. They simply can see energy in another dimension. It's not scary to those who understand it. People can be taught with the proper care to take control of this and understand it so their fear and anxieties are taken away. These gifted people don't need to be taking medications. They simply need guidance from a professional in that area.

My family and I are all gifted in different ways. Other than the blue orb, I don't see spirits but I have had many different experiences in having premonitions since I was twenty. I have also heard my intuition, higher self, whatever you choose to call it, speak to me in that gentle voice sometimes. Once it was explained to me in recent years by spiritual people who know what they are talking about, I understand it and no longer fear it. People are fearful of what they don't understand. They have to stop labelling gifted people as weird or crazy. I find it weird and crazy that more medical professionals don't take this reality more seriously.

I feel teaching meditation and yoga is something that really works for anxiety and other mental health issues as well. It would be so beneficial if it were taught to children from a young age. I would love to see all schools teaching these practices. It can calm down the brain overload. With all the technology children use nowadays it only makes them more stressed in my opinion and they need to find relief and practice daily, healthy, good habits.

Therapy is very important for good mental health. Mackenzie did have a therapist but her appointments were far apart and when she would be locked away in the hospital for thirty days, several times, there was no therapist provided for her to talk to. I feel she could have done better seeing someone more often right from the beginning when she first sought help. There seems to be a shortage of therapists. You are lucky if you get an appointment once a month or every two weeks at best. We need more help there.

There should never be guilt or shame attached to suicide victims or families. Every one of us fought for my granddaughter and fought with her as she did for herself. She was tired and I understand her despair. What I don't understand is the mental health system. I talked to an older police officer when I lived in Edmonton and we had a conversation about mental health. His words to me were, "Alberta has the worse mental health system in Canada."

My intention is never to scare anyone away from medications because they are useful when used properly but to make more people aware and to maybe look at other options as well for good mental health wellness.

MacKenzie made us proud in many ways for her kindness to others. Even in her death she gave her organs to help others live on with her generous and beautiful gift. Jeanna heard from

Keep Going

three recipients 4 months after Kenzie passed away. The Hope Foundation relayed messages to her from the recipients.

One young man wrote on a card of how grateful he was to have received one of Mackenzie's kidneys. He had been on dialysis three times a week and now he is doing much better and said he can travel outside the country. Something Kenzie always wanted to do was travel the world so I feel part of her is going with him. Another person received her other kidney and someone else received her lungs. All of them are very grateful to Kenzie and to our family for this life changing gift!

I find it both profound and ironic how other families rejoice while our family is left to grieve and yet I feel a great sense of pride for my granddaughter and happiness for the recipients that get to live on because of her gift. Something wonderful came out of a tragedy. I send many blessing to those families who received my beautiful granddaughter's organs. Me and my family wish them all well. I know they are surely grateful for MacKenzie's kind soul.

Kenzie made us so proud of her for being in the Army Cadets from the age of 14 to 17 and graduating high school at 17. When covid came she had to give up the Cadets. She loved being a part of the organization so much.

We are so proud of her kind and loving heart to all creatures big and small as they loved her. She often volunteered at the animal shelter. Many times she would face time us with animals in her arms. On one of those calls there were ten German Shepherd puppies jumping all around her, all anxiously waiting for their chance for her to hold them. The ones she was holding in her arms were all licking her face and nibbling on her. These were her happiest moments. Her face was always lit up! That's how I remember her now. She had a soft spot for animals and she was always very kind to the underprivileged and the homeless.

MacKenzie was artsy and musically talented. Her favourite band in the world was Queen. Anyone that knew her knew about it. She talked about Queen all the time.

Kenzie had many friends and family show up to her memorial in May 2024. The room was filled with tears and love. I wrote her eulogy and read it. I didn't think I could get through it but I'm glad I did it for her and our family that I love so much. I know she was there with us that day. I could feel her presence in the room.

On April 10th, the second day that Kenzie had been on life support, I went home to rest before heading to Edmonton. I did an hour of meditation. It helps me tremendously to keep it together while under stress. While I was meditating with my broken heart I talked to her in my thoughts. I asked "Where are you Kenzie? Can you hear me?" My eyes were closed and still wet from crying. I suddenly saw a bright, golden light with white clouds in it. I focused in amazement and could see something appearing in the center of this vision. Slowly it became very clear. It was a beautiful white fluffy bird. It was just flapping its wings slowly and gliding in the golden light. I was amazed by this vision and opened my eyes for a second to make sure I wasn't dreaming. When I closed my eyes again I could still see it. This lasted only about 8 to 10 seconds and then it disappeared.

I feel strongly the vision was Kenzie communicating to me that she was at total peace and free from all pain. I felt some peace in that moment. The bird was a symbol to me and our family for how she felt, finally being free from all suffering. Although her body was still alive at that time I do believe much of her soul had already left and she was already in the light. She didn't want to come back to more of the same or worse and she is definitely not to blame for that.

This is certainly not the great romantic, love story ending I was hoping to have for this book. However, there is no greater love to me than my children and grandchildren and it is why this is such a sad and heartbreaking ending for me and my family. I wish it was something more uplifting and joyful. I do feel it is an important story to share.

The only positives I can see at this time in sharing this tragedy and great loss in our lives, if there is any, is that telling my granddaughter's story might save another life and might help people who have gone through the same kind of loss to not feel alone. I would also like to lift any shame that some might carry because of the way their loved one passed away. Suicide is often judged.

Mental illness is a disease, no different than a loss from any other disease. We carry no shame in my granddaughter's choice. Like I said, I know she wasn't her true, healthy self. We carry the same grief as any other family who lost a child from any illness. MacKenzie gave us plenty of reasons to be proud of her and that will never change for us and how we now remember her.

I feel helping others this way would make Kenzie happy and if nothing else brings her peace and some kind of justice. Sharing her story and how much we love her is certainly worthwhile. She was more than worthy!

Something that we are all grateful for is that Kenzie didn't die right away. We as a family got to spend nine days of loving her and saying our goodbyes. Not everyone gets that chance. I think this helped our family tremendously, especially her mom and dad. I can't imagine her leaving suddenly without that opportunity. So thank you God for that.

Probably the most important thing I have learned so far in this 3D life is that our physical bodies will die but our spirits never will. We live on into the next school of experiences and lessons. I will move through this pain and heartache and carry on living my best life for my granddaughter until I get to see her and hug her again. I have no doubt that will happen. I have faith our whole family will do the same.

My God is a loving and forgiving God and I believe Kenzie is gone back home and safe in God's loving arms. Fly free my angel. We will stay strong and keep going for you our beautiful Mackenzie Gabrielle. Until we meet again we will miss you daily and cry for you in our hearts. We will miss your quirky ways that made us smile. We will stay in the beautiful memories you have created for us for over twenty years, rather than the heartbreaking ones we wish we could have taken away. That won't service any of us well.

Forgiving the mistakes of others is also very important for me and my family. Plus letting go of thinking we could have done more. We all did our very best as Kenzie did. We do not intend to live in anger. As I wrote about already at great length, forgiveness is the key to living a good quality of life.

May all of your sunsets be as beautiful as you are sweetheart. We love you forever and always. xo

Diane M. Waterman

Again, the national suicide prevention number in Canada is 988. Keep Going!

MacKenzie Gabrielle
December 31ˢᵗ 2003 - April 18ᵗʰ 2024

ABOUT DIANE

I was born on September 25th 1956 in the town of Gander, Newfoundland and Labrador. My parents were Eric and Viola Waterman (Peckford). My family moved a few times when I was a child. My siblings and I were raised in Gander, Goose Bay, Clarke's Head and then my parents moved back to Gander when I was finished high school. I ended up going back to Goose Bay where my oldest sister was then living with her husband. I met a man and got married by the time I was 21.

In 1978 my two sisters and I, our spouses and young children moved to Fort McMurray, Alberta, Canada. Eventually our youngest sister and brother moved here as well. In 1997 I divorced my ex-husband and started working in the jewelry business for the next fifteen years. In 2011 I was diagnosed with fibromyalgia and couldn't work on my feet all day anymore. I retired and took up writing. It is something that quickly became a passion and has kept me busy.

Thank you all for your loving support over the past thirteen years with the release of all four books. It is deeply appreciated.

www.ingramcontent.com/pod-product-compliance
Lightning Source LLC
Chambersburg PA
CBHW070544010526
44118CB00012B/1218